Cycling through Georgia

Tracing
Sherman's March
from Chickamauga
to Savannah

*By Sue C. Bailey
and William H. Bailey, Ph.D.*

SUSAN
HUNTER
Atlanta, Georgia

Published by Susan Hunter Publishing, Inc.
Atlanta, Georgia

Manufactured in the
United States of America

5   4   3   2   1

Publisher: Susan Hunter
Editor: Phyllis Mueller
Editorial Assistant: Deavours Hall
Typesetting: Repro Services, Inc.
Design: Kathy Couch
Photographs: The Bailey Family

Cover illustration courtesy of Bailey Biking
Adventures

Library of Congress Cataloging-in-
Publication Data:

Bailey, Sue C., 1945-
    Cycling through Georgia : tracing
Sherman's march / by Sue C. Bailey and
William H. Bailey.
        p.   cm.
    ISBN 0-932419-23-2 : $8.95
    1. Historic sites—Georgia—Guide-books.
2. Georgia—Description and travel—1981-—
Guide-books. 3. Cycling—Georgia—Guide-
books. 4. Sherman's March to the Sea.
5. Georgia—History—Civil War, 1861-1865—
Battlefields—Guide-books. 6. United States—
History—Civil War, 1861-1865—Battlefields—
Guide-books. I. Bailey, William H., 1944- .
II. Title.
F287.B35   1989   89-11036
917.58—dc20   CIP

Contents

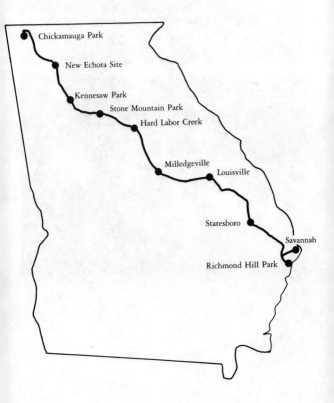

Chickamauga Park

New Echota Site

Kennesaw Park

Stone Mountain Park

Hard Labor Creek

Milledgeville

Louisville

Statesboro

Savannah

Richmond Hill Park

introduction

This book describes a unique bicycle route across Georgia. It facilitates planning for short and long distance touring along the approximately four hundred and seventy-five mile route. This guidebook is written for experienced and novice bicycle tourists. Sport and recreational riders will find the contents useful, as will visitors looking for an interesting automobile route through Georgia.

The hallmark of the route is its unifying theme, the march of General William T. Sherman's Union Army through Georgia in 1864. It is probably the most familiar event in the state's history. Pedaling along the Civil War route, the rider will discover and experience historical and contemporary Georgia. The cyclist will observe scenic landscapes and realize challenges and rewards posed by the state's varied terrain. Biking along the route also offers intimate contact with Georgia's cultural and natural environments.

The book presents a three-part tour corresponding to Sherman's three strategic movements. "The Atlanta Campaign" is approximately one hundred and ten miles long. It begins at the Chickamauga National Battlefield Park in Fort Oglethorpe, Georgia, and ends at Kennesaw National Battlefield Park in Marietta. The route continues with the "Siege of Atlanta," a forty-seven mile stretch through the capital city to Stone Mountain State Park. The final part follows the course taken by Sherman's left flank on the infamous "March to the Sea." It begins at Stone Mountain State Park and extends over three hundred miles to the historic city of Savannah. Focused on events of 1864, the route presents opportunities for fun, adventure, and learning which transcend its Civil War theme.

Georgia is a great place for bicycle touring. The year-round temperate climate provides many occasions for long distance tours during Spring, Summer, and Fall. The chief weather factor in those seasons is rain. Although winter precipitation and chilling winds inhibit safe cycling, there are enough relatively mild winter days for short adventures on the road.

The unifying theme of this route should inspire riders to complete their own "march," whether in short segments or on one grand tour.

foreword

Franklin Garrett, Historian of the Atlanta Historical Society and Official Historian of the City of Atlanta and of Fulton County, is an experienced bicycle traveler. When he heard about Cycling Through Georgia, *he shared these recollections of his bicycle days.*

FRANKLIN GARRETT'S BICYCLE DAYS

On September 25, 1918, the occasion of my twelfth birthday, I received my first bicycle — one that could be ridden long distances and not just on the sidewalk around the block. It was a *Niagra* equipped with a *Morrow* coaster brake and geared so that I could get up considerable speed without my legs going around very fast. Speed was regulated by the muscles in my legs rather than a number of gadgets mounted on the handlebars.

At that time I was living with my parents and sister in Atlanta, on 13th Street between Peachtree Street and Piedmont Avenue, only a short block from Piedmont Park.

When I received my bicycle, World War I was still going strong in Europe and Camp Gordon at Chamblee was going full blast. So, for my first fairly long ride, I rode to Camp Gordon, twelve miles to the north out Peachtree Road. At that time the paving on Peachtree Road ended at the DeKalb County line, though it was a good dirt road from that point on.

In August 1927 I decided to ride my bicycle to Baltimore, Maryland, via Richmond, Virginia and Washington. My Father was born and raised in Richmond and my Mother, though born in Washington, spent much of her girlhood in Baltimore.

At the time of this expedition we were living on 15th Street at the corner of Lombardy Way. I got started early and spent the first night in Anderson, South Carolina. From there I rode to Greenville, South Carolina and followed the Southern Railway Mainline through South Carolina, North Carolina and Virginia as far as Danville. From there I struck out in a northeasterly direction to Richmond. I spent the night before reaching Richmond at South Boston, Virginia. I stayed in Richmond a couple of days then rode to Washington via Fredericksburg. The busiest stretch of road was between Washington and Baltimore, a distance of forty miles. Few, if any, inter-city trucks impeded my progress.

After a couple of days in Baltimore, I returned to Washington and, my two weeks vacation

having expired, I caught the train home. I put my bicycle in the baggage car of the Piedmont Limited and, upon arrival at the Terminal Station in Atlanta, walked up to the baggage car, retrieved my bicycle and rode home.

Beginning in 1930 I started my self-imposed, unpaid project of recording Atlanta area cemeteries — those within a 30-mile radius in all directions from downtown Atlanta. In those years I was working for Western Union Telegraph Company and did lots of night work; hence, the time for cemetery recording.

I bought my first automobile, a brand new, gun-metal Ford with red wire wheels, with my own money. (In fact it did not occur to me while growing up that my Father should buy me a car when I achieved the age of 16. It did not occur to him, either!) So, with the purchase of my 1935 Ford (at the time, I was nearly 28) I gave up bicycling and gave my wheel to our once-a-week handy man.

Thus ended my bicycle era.

Franklin M. Garrett

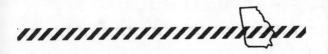

information

The idea for tracing Sherman's march by bicycle evolved during the 1970s. We joined the nationwide bicycling fad in 1972 and purchased ten speeds. Soon William's cycling focus shifted from recreation to commuting between home and the high school where he taught. He long had made local community field trips an integral part of his geography courses. Gradually, he replaced traditional walking and bus tours with more effective and efficient bicycle excursions. The success and popularity of these classtime rides led to longer student trips on weekends. The stage was set for what was to come.

How the Route Was Developed

While on summer vacation in 1978, our family met a group of young cyclists touring along the Kancamagus Highway in New Hampshire's White Mountains.

They were en route from Detroit to Acadia National Park in Maine. After a brief exchange with members of that group, William decided to plan a bicycle trip for students to trace Sherman's infamous march through Georgia. On such a trip they might learn first hand about the significant people, places, and events of historical and contemporary Georgia. And they would have the time of their lives doing it.

He proposed the trip as an interdisciplinary course with learning objectives in social studies, earth science, and physical education. Curriculum directors in his school system were fascinated by the prospects of this course. But the school system's attorney decided that the trip posed too great a liability risk. This opinion by the legal counsel did not deter William, however. All he needed to make the proposed trip was a support van, a driver, and some student riders willing to pay their expenses for a scholarly learning adventure without school credit.

Our first trip

In July of 1980, we made the first trip. General Motors Corporation generously donated a new Chevy Sport Van. Sue organized and managed logistical details and drove the van. Our two daughters, then aged nine and three, competently accompanied and assisted her. Eight adventurous and energetic youngsters, two girls and six boys ranging from eighth graders to high school seniors, comprised the pioneer group. From the start

2

it was obvious that the group would achieve the scholarly objectives. But we could not envision the personal rewards we all would gain from our inaugural trip.

The first step in planning the route was a review of the great variety of pertinent literature. We used the descriptions and easy-to-read maps in Samuel Carter's *The Siege of Atlanta* and Burke Davis's *Sherman's March* to sketch a general outline of the route. Another useful book is *Georgia Historical Markers*. This book contains the titles, complete texts, and precise locations of historical markers posted along Georgia's roadways. We reviewed the markers which chronicle Sherman's military actions and plotted their locations on topographic and county highway maps. Throughout this process we looked for and identified significant locations and patterns in the state's natural and cultural environment. This analysis helped us determine points of interest along the route.

Considerations

Rider safety and theme authenticity were foremost considerations in locating the route. Where possible, we planned the route to follow backroads that are lightly travelled, paved, and relatively smooth. The wide path cut across the state by Sherman's troops contains numerous alternatives suitable for safe cycling. Following the pattern of historical markers already plotted, we identified appropriate roads for the route. We evaluated traffic density and road quality by touring each mile both by car and bicycle. Finally, we chose a route to maximize rider safety and historical and contemporary significance. We have repeated this planning process each year since 1979 and have improved the route with appropriate changes.

How to Use This Guide

The guide presents the three parts of the route as they correspond to General Sherman's strategic movements in the state. For each part, a preview discussion introduces the historical and contemporary significance of the area, identifying major points of interest and important features. Each part is divided into segments. A segment is a section of the route which we recommend for one day of bicycle touring. Segments begin and end at places relevant to the route theme and are not loop rides. The segment name consists of its beginning and ending points.

Organization

Information essential for tour planning is presented for each segment. Some repetition was necessary so that the guide may be used for tours along the entire route or along a segment or part of it. *Length* is given in miles and kilometers. Riders may add dis-

tance to a segment by taking side trips to significant locations near the route and by touring within the small towns along the way. *Terrain* characteristics imply how physically demanding the ride may be and suggest the type of scenery to be observed. *Road surface, traffic*, and *hazards* are described to enhance rider safety. We have taken great care to locate roads which pose a minimum of hazards to bicyclers. Camping and motel *accommodations* are available at either end of a segment. These and other services of importance to bicycle tourists are noted. Where appropriate, specific establishments are recommended. The *population of central places* along the way implies the availability of services. The numbers were taken from 1980 census data.

Directions

Annotated lists of directions are keyed to a series of easy-to-read strip maps for each segment. The title of a map consists of the number representing the route part, the segment number for that part, and the map number for that segment. For example, *Map 1·1·4* is the fourth map in segment one of the first part of the route. The directions for each map are printed adjacent to the map. Listed in the directions are locations of turns, key points of interest, specific safety precautions, and touring suggestions. The distance between each item listed in the description is given in miles and kilometers. The number of each direction in the list matches the same number on the corresponding strip map. There is space on both the directions and map pages for the rider to make notes. If your experience touring along this route is anything like the ones we have had, you will make numerous notes about the people, places, and events you encounter along the way.

To the Novice Bicycler

Every bicycle touring book we have reviewed includes information about equipment and riding techniques for bicycle touring. Because we want a wide variety of people to use this book — the experienced bicycle tourist, the beginner, the sport and recreation cyclers, and adventurous students of Georgia who are looking for an effective way to learn about our state — we choose to include the following discussion. It is intended primarily for those who have little or no experience with bicycle touring but who wish to learn more about it before attempting this route. But we recommend that experienced bicycle tourists also read it.

The first thing we advise you to do is to join the League of American Wheelmen (LAW). (The address is listed in Appendix B.) LAW, the national organization of bicyclists, was founded in 1880. It protects the rights and promotes the interests of bicyclists, provides information about bicycling for its members and others, serves a nationwide network of affiliated bicycling clubs and organizations, and sponsors bicycle rallies and other bicycling activities. The organization's Bicyclists' Educational and Legal Foundation uses donations and grants to fund other programs. For its members, LAW publishes the *Bicycle USA* magazine nine times a year and, each January, the *Bicycle USA Almanac*. Bicycling resources listed in the *Almanac* and in the various issues of *Bicycle USA* are valuable for both novice and experienced bicycle tourists. We encourage you to consult these information sources.

Equipment

Essentials for making the trip described in this book are 1) a ten (or more) speed bicycle in good working order, 2) a hardshell bicycle touring helmet, 3) a water bottle, 4) a bicycle mounted bag, and 5) tire repair accessories including a pump, air gauge, extra tubes, and a tube patch kit. In each case, quality is the key ingredient for long term benefit. The inital cost for these items may seem high, but we hope biking will continue to be a rewarding form of exercise and travel for those who experience our ride.

There is a plethora of information about how to choose the right bicycle. Appropriate books and magazines are available in the public library and bookstores. We suggest that you review some of this material and then visit a reputable bicycle shop. The main concern is getting a bicycle that fits your body size. Be willing to wait for the dealer to order a suitable bicycle for you, if what you want is not in stock. (Remember, this vehicle can last for decades.) A multi-speed bicycle will enable you to negotiate hills with ease and to cruise effortlessly along the flatlands. Twelve, fifteen, and eighteen speed models are available. We recommend a standard, narrow-tire bicycle over the all-terrain style bike for this route. But either will suffice, if in good working order.

If you already have a bicycle, take it to a shop for a complete tune-up. Again, you may have to spend some money, but you will save yourself time and headaches down the road. There are very few bicycle shops in rural Georgia. Makeshift parts can be put together at hardware stores, but expert repairs are rarely available. Start your trip in good shape to avoid inconvenience and delays.

While at the bike shop, tell the owner your plans for this ride. Ask if you can observe the replacement of a tire and tube, since you are very likely to be doing this task somewhere on the road. It is also good to know how to change and adjust gear and brake cables. You should know how to repair or replace a broken chain. Your bicycle shop mechanic can suggest the tools you will need for these repair operations.

Every rider should strap on a bicycle helmet before every ride. It provides protection against head injury, if you should fall from your bike or if a missile comes your way. It will also attract the attention of motorists with whom you must share the road. We recommend a white, hardshell touring style helmet for safety and comfort. White reflects the intense summer sun, and vents on these models enhance cooling air flow. Some helmets have an adjustable sun visor which can serve you well.

A water bottle mounted to the bicycle is necessary in all weather, especially in the heat of the summer. The non-insulated kind holds more water and is lighter in weight. You should be able to open the bottle with your teeth — the "Look, Ma, no hands" riding trick is unwise on thin-wheeled bikes. In addition to containing refreshing water or juice, the bottle may be used as a defense against dogs. These critters usually withdraw when squirted.

Bicycle bags and the accompanying racks constitute another rather large expense. Begin with a small bag that hangs from the seat and does not require a rack. In this one bag you can carry essential items such as small tools, spare tubes, maps, sunscreen, first aid kit, bug repellent, money, and identification. If you wish to carry more items, you may need a set of bags (called panniers) which are mounted to a rack over the rear wheel of the bicycle. They can permit you to travel independent of a support vehicle by carrying camera, food, extra clothing such as rain gear and a swimsuit, and towels. They provide storage, for example, for extra layers of clothing and souvenirs.

Tire accessories are necessary. It is a good idea to check the pressure in the tires at regular intervals during the day. Low pressure causes drag and makes riding much more energy consuming.

Avoid being overwhelmed by all the available accessories. Bicycle shops and catalogs can make you feel like a kid looking at irresistable toys. After you have ridden your bicycle for a while and have gained experience, you will know better what accessories will provide more comfort and satisfaction for your individual style and purposes for cycling.

Clothing

You do not need expensive riding attire. Ordinary clothing will do quite well. There are, however, a few considerations when getting dressed to ride. The most fundamental concern is to be visible to motorists. Wear bright colors. Take care that your clothing cannot get tangled in the wheels, gears, or cable wires. Wear pants that fit tight at the ankles, or bind blousey bottoms with elastic. Consider weather conditions and body friction when dressing to bike. A sunny day may end with a sudden thunder shower. Sunscreen and clothing that covers tender areas will prevent pain and discomfort from sun and wind burn. Crucial body areas to protect are the

seat, thighs, and feet. Avoid shorts or pants with seams that will rub against your seat or thighs. Comfortable tennis shoes are fine for riding. Take an extra pair in case of rain. Soggy socks and shoes are heavy and uncomfortable.

Camping

If you choose to camp on your bicycle tour, you will need a tent to keep out rain and insects. Cool weather sleeping is most comfortable in a sleeping bag. However, in the heat of summer we prefer just a pad and some lightweight covers. If you choose to cook in camp, you will need a stove, fuel, matches, pots, pot holders, utensils, flatware, and dishes. You may wish to purchase lightweight varieties of these items to carry on your bicycle. We recommend, if you plan to camp, you carry your camping gear in a support vehicle. Remember that rural grocery stores may have limited varieties of foods. Plan your meals accordingly. Pasta and other carbohydrate foods store well and provide energy for the biker.

Costs

When planning your ride, you can estimate costs per day for you and each person travelling with you. Expenses will include food (camp-cooked or at restaurants), nightly accommodations (camping or motel), laundry, and fees for swimming, historic tours, bike repairs, incidentals, and souvenirs.

There will be transportation costs for getting to the starting point and returning home. Renting a vehicle to get back home is relatively inexpensive when compared to having a support vehicle accompany you every mile.

Tips and Safety

Most of us grew up riding a bicycle in our neighborhood. Bumps, bruises, and flat tires were easily cared for. This will not be the case on lightly travelled country roads. You could be miles from even a small town when something happens to put you off your bicycle. We recommend that you always travel with another biker. If you are a beginner, we urge you to have a support vehicle accompany you. We plan most of our trips that way. The daily segments in this book are not loop rides. They begin and end at places that have overnight accommodations. Those travelling in the support vehicle can easily go ahead and scout for places to eat, buy groceries, do laundry, and set up camp or get a motel room. This will leave the rider to enjoy the trip without the worry of time-consuming logistics.

There are many tips for safe riding. Ride only in daylight and try to avoid prolonged riding in the rain. Visibility is a critical factor in being safe on the roadway. Slippery road conditions create hazards for both cyclists and motorists. Take frequent rest stops. The small grocery stores scattered along the route provide nourishment for body and soul. Asking

questions often will generate an impromptu lesson in agricultural economics or local lore.

Always ride to the right and as close to the road edge as is safe. Watch for drop off road shoulders. If you go off the road and the shoulder is extreme, stop and lift your bicycle back on to the pavement. Listen for vehicles approaching from the rear. There are several times when getting off the road is a good idea: when there is traffic coming from both directions on a narrow road, when there is an oversized vehicle passing you either way, when there are vehicles backed up behind you on a long hill or bad curve. You may want to signal a stop and dismount until traffic has passed. Be alert to other types of hazards. Watch for vehicles entering the roadway from driveways and side roads, car doors opening in front of you, loose gravel, children, deep puddles, and dogs. The list goes on. Experience and being alert are your best defenses.

Training

Train for this ride, starting close to home. Ride where you are familiar with the conditions. This will give you a chance to test both your bicycle and your riding skills. You may also discover other bikers who may become future companion tourists. Do not avoid hills. Get off your bicycle and push it up hills until you master your gears. Pedaling up hills will become easy for you. As you build up your mileage capabilities, venture out along those portions of the route described in this book which are close to your home. Reading the directions and maps can be practiced on these jaunts. You may decide that other pieces of equipment will be handy on the longer ride.

A key factor to enjoying the full day rides is stamina. You should become able to ride ten miles on varied terrain without stopping. After ten miles, stop and take a short break. Then ride ten more miles. If you do this several days in a row, you should be able to make the entire trip with ease.

We have successfully led various groups along this route. Bikers from age ten to over sixty have pedaled the entire route with us and are proud of their accomplishment. You do not have to be an athlete to enjoy touring along this route. There are, of course, discrepancies in speed and endurance among age groups and individuals. After a few miles of riding, you will establish compatibility, and find a buddy.

For you who are just getting into biking, this route and book will provide a great start. The history, scenery, and people of Georgia invite your discovery.

PART

1

The Atlanta Campaign

Chickamauga National Battlefield Park to Kennesaw National Battlefield Park

(Approximately 110 Miles or 183 Kilometers)

The route begins at the Chickamauga National Battlefield Park in the Appalachian Ridge and Valley region of northwest Georgia. In September 1863, over 34,000 Americans died here in one of the bloodiest battles of the Civil War. A brochure available at the Visitor Center describes a seven-mile tour of the battlefield. The park area exists much the same as it was in 1863 and is a beautiful place for relaxed cycling. Of particular interest are the monuments erected after the war by veterans of the battle to com-

Chickamauga

memorate the men who fought in the bloody
action. Inscriptions on several mouments im-
plore mankind to avoid the madness of war.

The Battle of Chickamauga was prelude to
Sherman's Atlanta Campaign. After Chickamauga, the Confederate Army of 65,000 men
retreated south to Dalton. In May 1864, Sherman launched his force of 100,000 men on the
campaign to capture the Confederate manufacturing and railroad center at Atlanta. He
planned to follow the Western and Atlantic
Railroad to the objective over one hundred
miles away. As his main force drove at the en-
trenched and greatly outnumbered Confederates, he sent fast moving cavalry units on
flanking movements to threaten the enemy's
rear guard. The Confederates reacted with a
series of retreats to avoid being outflanked
and cut off from rear support. These maneuvers culminated in the Battle of Kennesaw
Mountain in June 1864.

From Chickamauga Park the bicycle route
leads eastward to Ringgold, where Sherman
began the Atlanta Campaign. The old Western and Atlantic Railroad Depot bears evidence
of war action in the city. Its 14-inch thick
sandstone walls were badly damaged by artil-
lery fire. Their repair with limestone blocks
shows an eerie contrast. An attempt has been
made to convert this relic to a museum. (The
varied fates of depots all along the route are
notable.)

During the 1930s, the Works Progress Ad-
ministration constructed a series of historical

monuments commemorating strategic actions in the Civil War. One of them is located in a roadside park along the route beyond the railroad depot in Ringgold. Like most of these memorials, it is poorly maintained. But it elaborately portrays the movements of the opposing armies in this area.

The route turns south at Ringgold and goes through one of the elongated northeast trending valleys which, along with the ridges they separate, characterize this scenic region. The rural landscape and gently rolling valley terrain produce excellent riding conditions.

The small town of Tunnel Hill got its name from the railroad tunnel through a small hill at the edge of town. Although of limited significance in the war, this product of a freak engineering decision warrants the short trip to view it. The route skirts the city of Dalton, carpet capital of the world, and continues through the rural valley to the village of Villanow. At this antebellum crossroads a group of local men are usually sitting on the steps of Penland's Country Store. This structure existed during the war and is one of many rural stores which are oases for bikers thirsting for drink and local lore.

A short distance east of Villanow is Snake Creek Gap, a narrow three-mile easterly passage between two north-south ridges. In a surprise night maneuver, Sherman led his main force from the Dalton front through this gap. To avoid being outflanked, the Confederates

withdrew southward to the village of Resaca. The bicycle route follows the gently rolling roads and scenic rural landscape from Villanow through the Snake Creek Gap to Resaca.

Resaca was the site of a significant skirmish between the two maneuvering armies. Historical markers located around the village detail the action, and a Confederate cemetery there commemorates the results. To avoid being trapped, the Confederates abandoned their position at Resaca, crossed the Oostanaula River, and moved south along the railroad to Adairsville. The bridge over the Oostanaula River at Resaca was the target of Andrews's Raiders in 1862, when the group of Union spies perpetrated the "Great Locomotive Chase" that was later eulogized by a Walt Disney movie. You'll find out more about this event in Kennesaw.

A few miles south of Resaca is the New Echota State Historic Site. New Echota was the seat of government for the Cherokee Indian Nation from 1825 to 1835. Located at the site are a museum of Indian culture and replicas of the first Indian-language newspaper office, a court house, a tavern, and the house of a Cherokee leader. The treaty which relinquished Cherokee claims to lands east of the Mississippi was signed there, and it became the assembly place of Indians for their removal west along the famous "Trail of Tears."

The bicycle route continues through the busy town of Calhoun which, like its neighbors Dalton to the north and Cartersville to the south, reflects the industrial growth in this region. The route follows a lightly travelled stretch of U.S. Highway 41 through the scenic and relatively flat Oothcaloga Valley to Adairsville, site of critical strategic decisions by the leaders of the opposing armies.

General Joseph E. Johnston, commander of the Confederate army, made a tactical maneuver at Adairsville which caused Sherman to divide his force into halves. The road bends southeast toward Cassville, but the railroad continues due south to Kingston. Johnston sent a small cavalry unit along the railroad to Kingston and led his main force along the road to Cassville. When Sherman reached Adairsville, he was unsure where the Confederates had gone. Consequently, as Johnston hoped, Sherman split his force sending one half to Kingston and the other to Cassville. Johnston deployed his troops at Cassville on the high ground overlooking the narrow valley into which Sherman's troops would come and waited to attack. At last, the Confederates would outnumber the Yankees in a battle. But Confederate General John Bell Hood failed to initiate the surprise attack, and Sherman's troops avoided the ambush. The Confederates retreated south toward Kennesaw Mountain, the last significant high ground to defend before Atlanta. The Civil War cemetery at Cassville contains the remnants of trenches in the Confederate position.

The bicycle route continues through Cassville and Cartersville toward Kennesaw Mountain. Antebellum and Victorian houses line the route as it enters Cartersville. South of this small industrial city at the Etowah River are the remains of a Civil War era bridge and a Confederate base camp. At this point, the route leaves the Ridge and Valley Region and enters the relatively hilly Piedmont. Lake Allatoona provides a scenic resting place, but it also marks the beginning of metropolitan Atlanta traffic.

The town of Kennesaw is the last stop on the route before the Kennesaw Mountain National Battlefield Park, and it is an interesting place. During the Civil War it was called Big Shanty and was a refueling stop for steam powered railroad locomotives. In 1862, Andrews's Raiders stole the locomotive the General while its crew and passengers were eating breakfast and resting at Big Shanty. Robert Fuller, a railroad employee, pursued the thieves on foot and eventually chased them with the locomotive the Texas. This was the story of the Great Locomotive Chase. The General is housed in the Big Shanty Museum in Kennesaw. Historical markers near the museum relate the story.

This major part of the route ends at the Kennesaw National Battlefield Park which commemorates the battle there in June 1864. A brochure available at the Museum and Visitor Center describes a self-guided vehicle tour of the battlefield park and its fifteen miles of hiking trails. The summit of Kennesaw Mountain may be reached along a foot trail and by road. We recommend biking to the top. On a clear day, the panoramic view from the summit includes the Atlanta skyline and historic Stone Mountain.

As a result of their defeat at Kennesaw, the Confederates retreated toward Atlanta. President Jefferson Davis relieved General Johnston of his command and replaced him with the impetuous General John Bell Hood. Meanwhile, Sherman planned for the Siege of Atlanta.

Villanow, Ga.

Directions:

PART 1 · SEGMENT 1

Chickamauga National Battlefied Park to New Echota State Historic Site

Length

Approximately 57.5 miles (92.5 kilometers)

Terrain

This segment of the route is in the Appalachian Ridge and Valley landsurface region. With a few exceptions, the route follows gently rolling valley roads. Some stretches are very level. There are a few moderate hills.

Road Surface

The roads are in good condition for bicycling. Most are smooth to coarse textured pavement. Throughout the state, road shoulders are inconsistent and generally dangerous.

Traffic

Traffic is moderately heavy along U.S. 27 from the Chickamauga Park Museum at the start of the route into the city of Fort Oglethorpe, along Georgia Highway 2 (Battlefield Parkway), and through the city of Ringgold. The short stretches along U.S. Highway 41 beyond Ringgold, at Tunnel Hill, and

23

through Resaca have moderate but highway-speed traffic. Tractor trailer trucks are common on U.S. 41. Georgia Highway 201 also has moderate and highway-speed traffic, but there are fewer trucks. The remainder of the route is along sparsely traveled rural roads.

Hazards

Exercise caution in each city and along each U.S. and State Highway. Tractor-trailor trucks are common along U.S. 41.

Accommodations

Fort Oglethorpe, Ringgold, Tunnel Hill, Villanow, and Resaca provide a variety of services. There are many motel accommodations located in the Fort Oglethorpe and Ringgold area at the start of the segment and in Calhoun near the end. There are no government-operated campgrounds along this segment except for primitive group camping at Chickamauga National Battlefield Park. There is a KOA campground at the intersection of Interstate Highway 75 and Ga. 2 (Battlefield Parkway) in Ringgold and another in Calhoun (see direction number 5 for Map 1·2·1 below). We recommend these sites if you plan to camp at either end of this segment. Be sure to make reservations as early as possible on the day you wish to stop for overnight accommodations. More advanced notice is usually not required.

Population of Central Places

Fort Oglethorpe - 5,443, Ringgold - 1,821, Tunnel Hill - 867, Resaca - 500.

Map 1·1·1

(0.0 miles) (0.0 kilometers)

Begin at the Chickamauga National Battlefield Park Museum. The Park Headquarters Office is located in this building. Go north on U.S. 27 (also called Lafayette Road) into the town of Fort Oglethorpe.

2 *(1.5) (2.4)*

At the intersection of U.S. 27 (Lafayette Road) and Ga. 2 (also called Battlefield Parkway) in Fort Oglethorpe, turn right (east) on to Ga. 2 (Battlefield Parkway). There is a traffic light at this intersection, and there is a Kmart in the shopping center on the right before the turn.

(6.5) (10.5)

On the left (north) along Ga. 2, before crossing I-75, is a KOA campground. Cross under Interstate Highway 75.

4 *(1.3) (2.1)*

At the stop sign where Ga. 2 (Battlefield Parkway) merges with U.S. 41 (also Ga. 3), turn right (south). Follow U.S. 41 south through the city of Ringgold.

5 *(1.5) (2.4)*

The old Western & Atlantic Railroad Depot is on the left. A historical marker titled

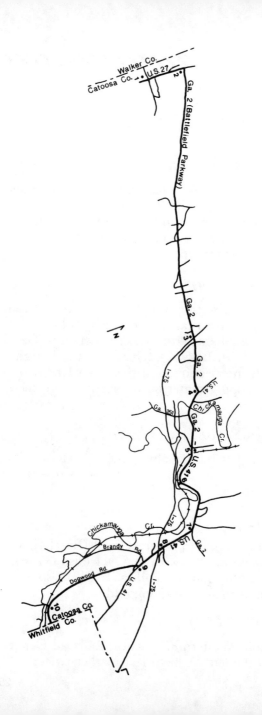

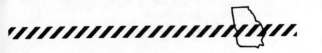

"Western & Atlantic Depot" is located on the site.

6 *(0.7) (1.1)*

The elaborate, but deteriorating, historical monument "The Battle of Ringgold" is located in the roadside park on the right. The monument was built by the WPA during the 1930s and depicts Civil War action prior to Sherman's campaign.

7 *(1.6) (2.6)*

Turn right (south) to remain on U.S. 41 (also Ga. 3), where it separates from Ga. 2.

8 *(0.9) (1.5)*

Cross over Interstate Highway 75.

9 *(0.7) (1.1)*

Turn right (west) on to Dogwood Road. Although this road is marked with a sign on a pole, you must take care not to pass it. This road bends southward through the Dogwood Valley.

10 *(2.5) (4.0)*

At the railroad tracks turn left (east) on to Campbell Road. The turn will appear to be a continuation of Dogwood Road, which leads to the south across the tracks. Do not cross the tracks. After the turn Campbell Road has a short, but steep, hill directly ahead.

Map 1·1·2

1 *(1.2 miles) (1.9 kilometers)*

Turn right (south) on U.S. 41 (Ga. 3)
and enter the town of Tunnel Hill. Be aware
that traffic on U.S. 41 can be heavy, especially in the towns. Tractor trailer trucks are
common and reflect the area's industrial deve-
lopment, particularly the carpet industry. The
main part of the old town of Tunnel Hill and
the railroad tunnel are located on the east side
of U.S. 41.

Directions inside Tunnel Hill: After turning on to U.S 41 from Campbell Road, begin looking for Ga. 201 which turns left off
of U.S. 41 a short distance into Tunnel Hill.
Follow Ga. 201 to the stop sign at Varnell
Road and turn right. At the stop sign you
will be in the heart of old Tunnel Hill. Turn
right and then back to the left to see the railroad tracks. At the tracks look to the left to
see the tunnel. The historical marker "Clisby
Austin House" is located on the left across the
tracks. Cross the tracks and continue on this
street which bends to the left and leads back
to U.S. 41. At U.S. 41, the historical marker
"Tunnel Hill" is posted on the left. Turn left
(south) on to U.S. 41.

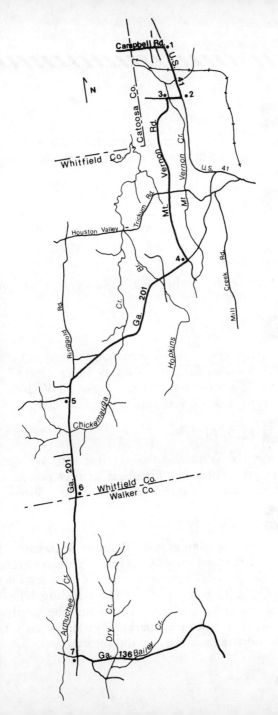

2 *(1.1) (1.8)*

South of the bridge over the railroad on U.S. 41, turn right (west) on to Cottonwood Mill Road.

3 *(0.5) (0.8)*

Turn left (south) on to Mount Vernon Road.

4 *(3.4) (5.5)*

At the traffic light, turn right (southwest) on to Ga. 201.

5 *(4.5) (7.2)*

There are two historical markers posted at Gordon Springs Road: "Callaway Place, 1814" and "Twentieth Corps in Dogwood Valley." Continue southwestward along Ga. 201.

6 *(2.0) (3.2)*

Cross the Whitfield County line into Walker County. There is a historical marker posted at this point: "Geary's Division to Dug Gap."

7 *(3.2) (5.1)*

At the stop sign at the village of Villanow, turn left (east) on to Ga. 136. Penland's store is on the southwest corner of the intersection of Ga. 201 and Ga. 136. The building housing the store was in place during the Civil War. The historical marker "Villanow" is on the northwest corner of the intersection.

Map 1·1·3

1 *(5.0 miles) (8.0 kilometers)*

This stretch of the route passes through the mouth of Snake Creek Gap. The road generally parallels the creek, but the two intersect at several points in the next four miles.

2 *(1.8) (2.9)*

Cross the Walker County line into Gordon County.

3 *(1.2) (1.9)*

Turn left (east) to remain on Ga. 136 toward Resaca. There is a sign pointing to Resaca. The road straight ahead is Ga. 136 Connector. On the left before the turn is the historical marker "Snake Creek Gap."

4 *(6.5) (10.5)*

Cross over Camp Creek and Interstate Highway 75. Between the creek and the highway there are two historical markers posted on the left: "Battle of Resaca" and Polk's Line Withdrawn to Resaca."

5 *(0.5) (0.8)*

Ga. 136 ends at U.S. 41 in the village of Resaca. Turn left (north) on to U.S. 41 to visit the Confederate Cemetery in Resaca. Be alert to the traffic on U.S. 41. Several historical markers posted in Resaca chronicle the events of the Battle of Resaca.

6 *(1.9) (3.1)*

A sign marks the road which leads to the Confederate Cemetery. Turn right on to this road. On the right at the turn in the Roadside Park is a historical monument built by the WPA in the 1930s. This monument describes the action in the Battle of Resaca.

7 *(0.5) (0.8)*

The Confederate Cemetery is on the right. The historical marker "Confederate Cemetery" describes the place. Return to U.S. 41 and turn left (south). Return to Resaca and cross the Oostanaula River Bridge.

8 *(2.5) (4.0)*

Turn left (east) on to the county road. This road marked with the number 483 posted on the stop sign where it meets U.S. 41. Cross the railroad tracks in a short distance.

9 *(2.7) (4.3)*

At the stop sign turn left on to Ga. 225. There is a golf course on the left. On the

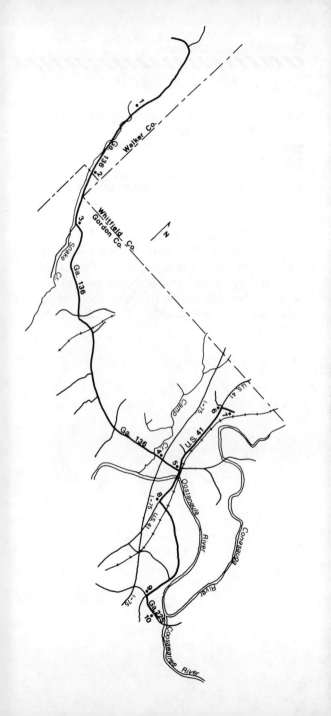

northeast corner of this intersection there is a historical monument.

10 *(0.4) (0.6)*

The New Echota State Historical Site is on the right.

Note: Although this segment of the route ends at New Echota State Historic Site, overnight accommodations are located a short distance further along at the beginning of Segment 2. For directions to these accommodations, see direction number 5 for Map 1·2·1.

Directions:

PART 1 · SEGMENT 2

New Echota State Historic Site to Kennesaw Mountain National Battlefield Park

Length
Approximately 55 Miles (88.5 kilometers)

Terrain
Most of this segment of the route is in the Appalachian Ridge and Valley landsurface region. South of Cartersville this region merges with the Piedmont. The route crosses gently rolling terrain with some moderate hills near the end of this segment.

Road Surface
The roads are in good condition for bicycling. Most are smooth asphalt, but there are some stretches of coarse textured pavement. Road shoulders are inconsistent and generally dangerous.

Traffic
Traffic is generally heavy in all of the towns along this segment. The stretches between Cal-

houn and Cartersville and from Cartersville to the Cobb County line are primarily rural, with sparse traffic. Beginning in Cobb County, however, generally heavy surburban traffic prevails. During the warm season, traffic around Lake Allatoona is heavy.

Hazards

Because of relatively heavy traffic, extreme caution is necessary in each city, in the suburban area of Cobb County, and at Lake Allatoona. Although Interstate 75 parallels this segment of the route, tractor-trailer traffic occurs on U.S. 41 and on state highways. The traffic at Lake Allatoona in the warm season poses the two-fold danger of people pulling boats on trailers and people driving under the influence of alcohol. Traffic density increases dramatically where the route enters Cobb County.

Accommodations

There are numerous stores located along this segment. Each town provides a variety of services. Between Acworth and Kennesaw Mountain National Battlefield Park in Cobb County the route passes several large shopping centers. Several bicycle shops located near the end of this segment are listed in the local yellow pages. Motel accommodations are abundant. Although there are no camping facilities at Kennesaw Mountain, there is a KOA campground located on the route two miles before the end of this segment (see direction number 7 for Map 1·2·4). Red Top Moun-

tain State Park is located a short distance off
the route before the end of this segment (see
direction number 7 for Map 1·2·3 below).

Population of Central Places
Calhoun - 5,335, Adairsville - 1,739,
Cartersville - 9,508, Emerson - 1,110,
Acworth - 3,648, Kennesaw - 5,095,
Marietta - 30,805.

Map 1·2·1

1 *(0.0 miles) (0.0 kilometers)*

From the New Echota State Historic Site, turn left (west) on to Ga. 225.

2 *(0.4) (0.6)*

Turn left (south) on to New Town Church Road.

3 *(0.8) (1.3)*

The historical marker "New Echota Cemetery" points out the location of the burial ground used by inhabitants of New Echota.

4 *(0.6) (1.0)*

Continue on New Town Church Road through this intersection.

5 *(1.0) (1.6)*

At the stop sign turn right (west) on to Ga. 156 (also called Red Bud Road).

Note: The Calhoun KOA campground is located approximately 1.5 miles to the east (left) on Ga. 156 (Red Bud Road) from this point. Motel and restaurant accommodations are located within one mile to the west (right) on the route along Ga. 156.

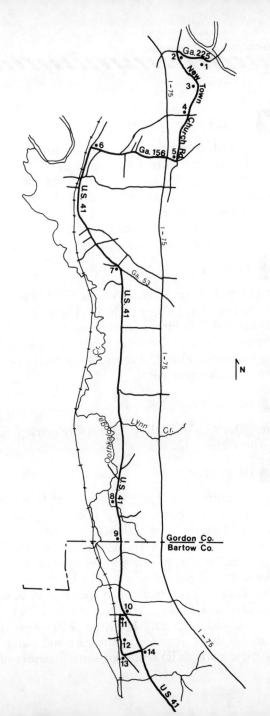

6 *(2.3) (3.7)*

At the traffic light where Ga. 156 joins U.S. 41 (also Ga. 3), turn left (south) on to U.S. 41. Proceed with caution through the city of Calhoun. There is no paved shoulder along this stretch. The route will lead you by the Gordon County Courthouse and through the Calhoun central business district.

7 *(2.9) (4.7)*

At the traffic light, U.S. 41 intersects Ga. 53. Remain on U.S. 41 south. There is a good paved shoulder from this point, but it is narrow. There are several large factories a short distance ahead, but the route will become increasingly rural.

8 *(4.7) (7.6)*

The "Oothcaloga Valley" historical marker is on the right.

9 *(0.9) (1.4)*

At this point, the route passes from Gordon County to Bartow County. The historical marker "Original Site Adairsville - 1830s" is on the right. On the right, parallel to the main road at this point, you will notice a stretch of roadway called the Old Dixie Highway. This was the main road many years ago. Old Dixie Highway, the current U.S. 41 (Ga. 3), and Interstate Highway 75 (which is located a short distance to the east and parallels these two roads) represent some measure of

progress in road building in the state. But the abandoned stores that you will see along U.S. 41 between here and Cartersville resulted largely from the relocation of intercity highway traffic to I-75. **Although the Old Dixie Highway may appear inviting to the bicycler, do not use it. It poses too many hazards, such as rough pavement, hidden driveways, and blind intersections.**

10 *(1.6) (2.6)*

At the traffic light, turn right (west) on to Ga. 140 for a short side trip into Adairsville.

11 *(0.2) (0.3)*

Turn left (south) on to North Main Street which leads into Adairsville.

12 *(0.6) (1.0)*

Turn right on to Park Square Street. The old railroad depot, now used for another purpose, is on the right. At the second stop sign, turn left. At South Main Street turn right.

13 *(0.3) (0.5)*

At the sign "To U.S. 41" turn left (east).

14 *(0.3) (0.5)*

At the stop sign turn right (south) on to U.S. 41. Directly across the highway from this stop sign is a cemetery with three historical markers: "Johnston's Army at Adairsville," "Federal Armies at Adairsville," and "Mosteller's Mills."

Map 1·2·2

1 *(8.6 miles) (13.8 kilometers)*

Just south of the bridge over Two Run Creek turn left (southeast) on to Cassville Road. The historical marker "Gravelly Plateau And Two Run Creek" is located near the southeast side of the bridge.

2 *(0.9) (1.4)*

Turn left (east) on to Cass-White Road. This is the center of the old town of Cassville. On the west side of Cassville Road at this turn there is a fire station. On the corner of Cassville Road and Cass-White Road the historical marker "Town of Cassville" is posted in the open space across from the fire station. Proceed with caution along the winding Cass-White Road to the Civil War cemetery.

3 *(0.5) (0.8)*

A Civil War cemetery is on the right at Shinall-Gaines Road. The historical marker "Confederate Dead" is posted at the entrance to the cemetery. On the high ground in the cemetery there are remnants of trenches dug by Confederate soldiers preparing to ambush Sherman's soldiers. Monuments and grave markers in the cemetery are memorials to the soldiers on both sides. After viewing this site, return to Cassville Road.

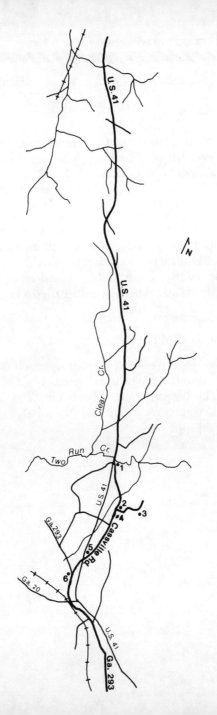

4 *(0.5) (0.8)*

Turn left (south) on to Cassville Road. Be careful to remain on Cassville Road as you pass several forks in the road.

5 *(1.2) (1.9)*

On the right at the intersection of Cassville Road and the 4-lane (U.S. 41) there is a historical monument site built by the WPA during the 1930s. Cross U.S. 41 and remain on Cassville Road, which is also called Ga. 293 Connector from this point.

6 *(0.4) (0.6)*

Turn left (south) on to Ga. 293, which is also called Cassville Road until it reaches Cartersville. The bicycle route follows Ga. 293 all the way to Kennesaw Mountain National Battlefield Park.

Map 1·2·3

1 *(4.2 miles) (6.8 kilometers)*

Use caution at the underpass. The Cartersville city limit sign is ahead a short distance.

2 *(1.5) (2.4)*

At the stop sign, Cassville Road ends. Turn left (east) on to Cherokee Avenue and follow the Ga. 293 South signs.

3 *(0.2) (0.3)*

At the stop sign, turn right (south) on to North Bartow Street.

4 *(0.1) (0.2)*

At the traffic light, turn left (east) on to North Main Street which will lead you into the Cartersville central business district and across the railroad tracks at the old depot.

5 *(0.3) (0.5)*

At the first traffic light beyond the railroad tracks which cross North Main Street, turn right (south) and follow Ga. 293 south toward Emerson. There are signs marking this turn.

6 *(1.1) (1.8)*

Use caution at the narrow underpass.

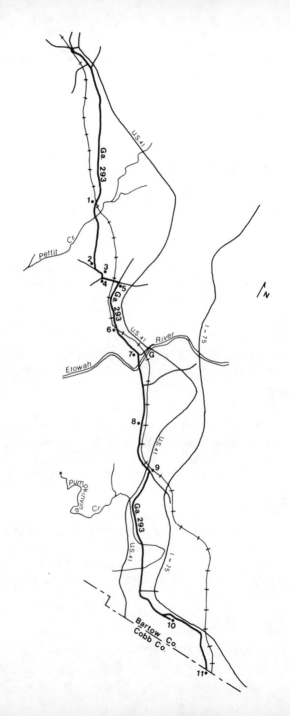

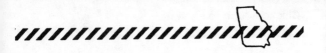

7 *(0.7) (1.1)*

Before reaching the Etowah River bridge, turn
left (east) and take a short ride to the site of
the remains of a Civil War era bridge across
the Etowah. It is on the right, a short distance east of the U.S. 41 bridge over the
river. On the hill north of the old bridge
is the site of a Confederate outpost. Return
to Ga. 293, turn left (south), and cross the
Etowah River bridge.

Note: If you wish to camp at Red Top Mountain State Park, turn left at the park direction sign located less than one mile south of
the Etowah River bridge on Ga. 293. Follow
the signs to the park. There will be several
turns before the park, but each is marked.

8 *(1.4) (2.3)*

The Emerson City Limit sign is posted on the
right. At this small town Sherman's soldiers
destroyed the railroad tracks and twisted the
heated rails around the trunks of trees. They
remained that way for many years as a
reminder of the war.

9 *(1.2) (1.9)*

Go under the U.S. 41 bridge and turn right
(south) to remain on Ga. 293. Signs mark
this turn which is located immediately beyond
the U.S. 41 overpass. Take care not to get on
to U.S. 41 and not to miss the turn to continue south on Ga. 293.

10 *(3.8 miles) (6.1 kilometers)*

On the right on the other side of this bridge over Lake Allatoona is a roadside park with lake access.

11 *(1.5) (2.4)*

Cross into Cobb County. Remember that traffic density will increase from this point.

Map 1·2·4

1 *(0.8) (1.3)*

Pass under the Ga. 92 bridge and proceed along Ga. 293 into the town of Acworth.

2 *(3.2) (5.1)*

North Cobb High School is located on the left.

3 *(1.5) (2.4)*

The Kennesaw city limit sign is posted on the right.

4 *(1.0) (1.6)*

The Big Shanty Museum is on the left. Note the series of historical markers posted along the roadside at the museum. Be sure to visit the museum and to view the markers.

5 *(1.8) (2.9)*

At the intersection of Ga. 293 and U.S. 41, cross U.S. 41 and continue on Ga. 293 (also called Old 41 Highway). A KOA campground is located on the left across U.S. 41.

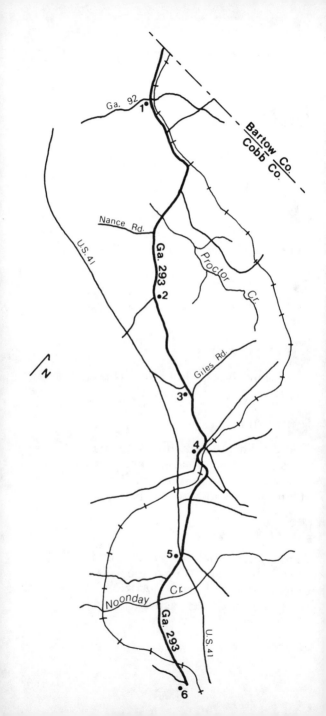

6 *(2.1) (3.4)*

Turn right on to Stilesboro Rd. The entrance to the Kennesaw National Battlefield Park and the Park Headquarters and Museum are on the left.

Kennesaw National Battlefield Park

2

The Siege of Atlanta

Kennesaw National Battlefield Park to Stone Mountain State Park

(Approximately 47 Miles or 76 Kilometers)

NOTE: We recommend cycling along this part of the route on a Sunday only. The usually heavy metropolitan Atlanta area traffic is at its minimum on Sunday.

Sherman led his main force from the Kennesaw Mountain battlefield toward Atlanta along the railroad. He deployed other units in various flanking maneuvers to the east and west of the city. This part of the route follows that of Sherman's main force and passes many significant places.

The Civil War era railroad depot area in the heart of Marietta has been restored. Converted to a restaurant, the depot attracts tourists and local residents. Historical markers posted on the site relate important events that occurred there. A short distance east and within view of the town square is the Marietta National Cemetery. It was created on land donated by a private citizen as a gesture of peace for interment of Civil War dead. Confederate families, however, refused to bury their fallen soldiers next to the Yankee dead. Thousands of white markers commemorate veterans from the Civil War era to present.

The approach to Atlanta crosses the Chattahoochee River. The retreating Confederates hastily established defensive lines along the Chattahoochee and a nearby tributary where a significant battle ensued. Historical markers located along the battle line chronicle the strategic encounter at the "Battle of Peachtree Creek." The short side trip to Peachtree Battle Avenue leads through one of Atlanta's most attractive older neighborhoods.

Two momentous events are memorialized by historical markers situated near Atlanta's central business district. The portentous transfer of the Confederate command from General Joseph E. Johnston to General John Bell Hood hastened the subject of another marker. Located at the intersection of Marietta Street and Northside Drive on the northwest edge of downtown Atlanta is the historical marker "Surrender of Atlanta: September 2, 1864."

The state capitol complex on the southeast side of Atlanta's central business district is a major attraction for visitors. Sherman's troops camped on these grounds after capturing the city. Remember, however, that during the Civil War Milledgeville was the state capital, not Atlanta. The story of the Battle of Atlanta is best told by the Cyclorama painting located a few blocks from the capitol in Grant Park. A viewing of this vivid representation of the fight for the city is essential to this tour. Housed in the Cyclorama building is the locomotive Texas, which was involved in the "Great Locomotive Chase" associated with Andrews's Raiders.

The actual site of the Battle of Atlanta is a short distance east of Grant Park. In this same area is the McPherson Memorial Monument, which marks the location where one of Sherman's most revered generals was killed in action. It was McPherson's cavalry unit that executed the crucial flanking movements from Ringgold to Kennesaw Mountain.

Atlanta is a big city with many attractions which go far beyond the scope of this bicycle route, but there are numerous sites along the route. Most of them are pertinent to the route's theme, but others are not. They include the Atlanta-Fulton County Stadium where monuments pay tribute to baseball greats Ty Cobb and Hank Aaron, the Martin Luther King, Jr., National Historic Site, the Civil War era Oakland Cemetery, and Little

Five Points, Atlanta's contemporary bohemia. You may wish to spend some time touring the many other attractions which this city has to offer before pedaling on toward the sea.

Leaving downtown Atlanta, the route continues eastward on Memorial Drive, which was named to honor Confederate veterans. Stone Mountain looms on the horizon. The unique feature of Stone Mountain State Park is the granite mountain with its huge carving of Confederate Generals Robert E. Lee and Stonewall Jackson and Confederate President Jefferson Davis. During spring and summer the park draws thousands of patrons to its attractions, which include a nightly laser show beamed on to the memorial carving.

Directions:

PART 2 · SEGMENT 1

Kennesaw National Battlefield Park to Stone Mountain State Park

Length
Approximately 47 miles or 76 kilometers

Terrain
This section of the route is in the Piedmont landsurface region. It is characterized by gently to moderately rolling terrain. There are a few short and steep hills.

Road Surface
All roads in this section have relatively smooth pavement. There is always road construction and repair, however, at various places in metropolitan Atlanta. Watch for typical urban road hazards, such as storm sewer grates, potholes, and resurfaced places where the street has been patched. Road shoulders are inconsistent, and elevated curbs are dangerous for cyclers.

Traffic
Traffic is this part of metropolitan Atlanta is heavy. We recommend that you cycle along

this segment of the route only on Sunday, when traffic is at a minimum. Even then, traffic can be relatively heavy at certain places and times of the day.

Hazards

Traffic is the major hazard. Georgia Highway 3 is somewhat narrow for the traffic volume it carries. The route from Smyrna into downtown Atlanta passes through a relatively continuous industrial zone. Tractor-trailer trucks will be present there even on Sunday. East of downtown Atlanta, along Memorial Drive, there are several places where railroad spur lines which serve old industrial sites pose hazards for cyclers. Occurrences of these crossings diminish with distance from the downtown area.

Accommodations

Motels abound at both ends and in the middle of this segment of the route. Camping is available at Red Top Mountain State Park located northeast of Kennesaw National Battlefield Park (see above) and at a KOA campground located on the route approximately two miles north of the Kennesaw National Battlefield Park Visitor Center. Stone Mountain State Park has a large family campground and several group camping sites. Every kind of service that the bicycle tourist would need is easily accessible from the route. Numerous bicycle shops are listed in the yellow pages of the telephone book. If you plan to spend some time

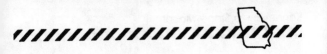

touring Atlanta, we recommend that you use the MARTA rail and bus system.

Population of Central Places
Marietta - 30,805, Smyrna - 20,312, Atlanta - 425,022, Stone Mountain - 4,867.

Map 2·1·1

1 *(0.0 miles) (0.0 kilometers)*

From the Visitors Center of Kennesaw National Battlefield Park turn right (south) on to Ga. 293, also called Old 41 Highway.

2 *(0.3) (0.5)*

Turn right (south) on to Kennesaw Avenue.

3 *(2.1) (3.4)*

Turn right (south) on to Church Street and proceed into downtown Marietta.

4 *(0.4) (0.6)*

At the traffic light at Roswell Street, the Marietta Square is on the left (east). Behind the row of buildings on the right is the old railroad depot. A short distance east along Roswell Street is the Marietta National Cemetery.

5 *(0.1) (0.2)*

Turn left (east) on to Waverly Way.

6 *(0.1) (0.2)*

Turn right (south) on to Atlanta Street.

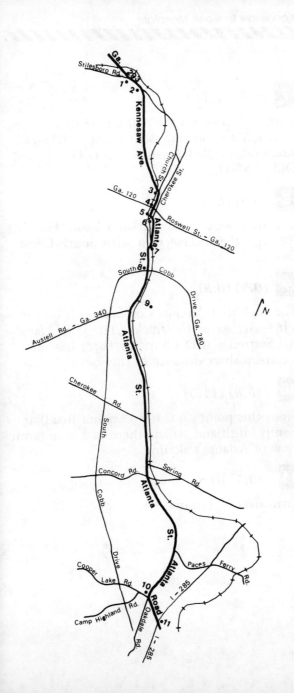

///////////////////////////

7 *(0.7) (1.1)*

Turn right to cross the railroad tracks and then turn left to continue south along Atlanta Road (also called Atlanta Street, Ga. 3, and Old U.S. 41).

8 *(0.5) (0.8)*

Continue south along Atlanta Road (Ga. 3) through the intersection with South Cobb Drive.

9 *(0.5) (0.8)*

The Lockheed Aircraft Corporation is on the left (east) across the tracks. The U.S. Naval Air Station and Dobbins Air Force Base are located a short distance to the south.

10 *(6.8) (11.0)*

From this point on Ga. 3 (Atlanta Road) at Camp Highland Road, there is a panoramic view of Atlanta's skyline.

11 *(0.5) (0.8)*

Cross over Interstate 285.

Map 2·1·2

(2.9 miles) (4.7 kilometers)

Cross over the Chattahoochee River and pass
from Cobb County into Fulton County.
After crossing the Chattahoochee River
Bridge, Ga. 3 is also called Marietta Boulevard. At the traffic light bear left (east) onto
De Foors Ferry Road for a short side trip to
visit the territory where the Battle of Peachtree
Creek was waged. This is a busy intersection
and can be confusing and dangerous. Stop and
survey it before proceeding. The roadway
which crosses Ga. 3 (Marietta Boulevard) is
called De Foors Ferry Road to the east and
Bolton Road to the west. Be sure to turn on
to De Foors Ferry Road. The Atlanta Water
Works complex is on the left.

(0.3) (0.5)

At the traffic light turn left on to Moores Mill
Road.

3 **(0.7) (1.1)**

Where Moores Mill Road crosses over Peachtree Creek, note the historical marker "Battle
of Moores Mill."

4 **(0.2) (0.3)**

At the caution light, turn right on to Peachtree Battle Avenue. This street passes through
historic ground and one of Atlanta's most
attractive residential areas.

5 *(0.8) (1.3)*

Note the historical marker "Green Bone Creek."

6 *(0.1) (0.2)*

Cross over Interstate Highway 75. This is a relatively new bridge. When it was under construction, a lot of battle relics were unearthed.

7 *(0.5) (0.8)*

Cross Howell Mill Road.

8 *(0.2) (0.3)*

Woodward Way, to the right, goes along Peachtree Creek through Atlanta Memorial Park. The park contains much of the Battle of Peachtree Creek battleground along the creek. Woodward Way meets Peachtree Battle Avenue again approximately 0.6 miles west of Peachtree Street. If you take Woodward Way, skip to direction number 11 below.

9 *(0.3) (0.5)*

Note the historical marker "Geary's Division to Peachtree Creek."

10 *(0.1) (0.2)*

Cross Northside Drive (also U.S. 41). Remain on Peachtree Battle Avenue, which angles to the right after crossing Northside Drive. Do

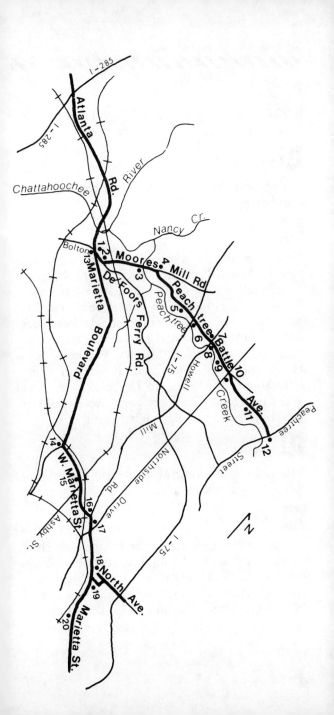

not confuse it with Manor Ridge Drive, which
is straight ahead at the intersection.

(0.7) (1.1)

Woodward Way is the street to the right (see
number 8).

12 *(0.6) (1.0)*

Peachtree Battle Avenue ends at Peachtree
Street. Across Peachtree Street is the Peachtree Battle Shopping Center which has a variety of services including banks, restaurants,
grocery stores, and a bookstore. At Peachtree
Street, turn around and retrace the route to
Marietta Boulevard as follows: Peachtree Battle Avenue to Moores Mill Road and turn
left, Moores Mill Road to De Foors Ferry Road
and turn right, De Foors Ferry Road to Marietta Boulevard and turn left (south).

(4.5) (7.2)

Proceed south along Marietta Boulevard toward downtown Atlanta.

14 *(3.2) (5.1)*

At the traffic light across the bridge over the
Inman Yard railroad complex, turn left (southeast) on to West Marietta Street. This area is
part of Atlanta's inner city fringe characterized
by old industrial sites and dilapidated housing.

15 *(0.6) (1.0)*

On the right is the historical monument and marker "Confederate Army Command Change."

16 *(0.6) (1.0)*

West Marietta Street merges with Marietta Street. Bear to the right and proceed southeast along Marietta Street.

17 *(0.2) (0.3)*

On the left at the intersection of Marietta Street and Northside Drive (U.S. 41) is the historical marker "Surrender of Atlanta: September 2, 1864." Cross Northside Drive and continue on Marietta Street.

18 *(0.7) (1.1)*

Cross over North Avenue. There is no access to North Avenue at this point, and you will be routed back to it. On the left is the corporate headquarters complex of the Coca-Cola Company.

19 *(0.2) (0.3)*

To visit the Coca-Cola complex, Georgia Tech, and the Varsity restaurant turn left (east) on to Pine Street. Travel 0.1 mile to Luckie Street and turn left (north). The Techwood Homes public housing neighborhood is on the right. Go 0.1 mile to North Avenue. Where

Luckie Street crosses North Avenue, the Coca-Cola complex is to the left (west) along North Avenue, and the Georgia Institute of Technology (Georgia Tech) complex is to the right (east). To the right (east) at 0.4 miles North Avenue crosses over Interstate Highway 75. The Varsity restaurant, home of great chili dogs, is on the left just beyond the intersection. Retrace the route to Marietta Street as follows: North Avenue to Luckie Street and turn left (south), Luckie Street south to Pine Street and turn right (west), Pine Street to Marietta Street and turn left (south).

20   *(0.6) (1.0)*

Georgia's World Congress Center and the Omni arena are located on the right.

Map 2·1·3

1 *(0.5 miles) (0.8 kilometers)*

Five Points is in the heart of the Atlanta central business district. Marietta Street ends (or begins) at Five Points. Bear to the right and continue along Decatur Street for one city block to Pryor Street.

2 *(0.1) (0.2)*

Turn right (south) on to Pryor Street. You will pass the Fulton County Courthouse which will be on the left and will cross Martin Luther King, Jr. Drive.

3 *(0.3) (0.5)*

Turn left (east) on to Mitchell Street. Cross Central Avenue. The Atlanta City Hall is ahead on the right. Cross Washington Street. The Georgia State Capitol building is on the left.

4 *(0.2) (0.3)*

Turn right (south) on to Capitol Avenue.

5 *(0.1) (0.2)*

Capitol Avenue intersects Memorial Drive (Ga. 154).

6 *(0.5) (0.8)*

Before turning left (east) on to Memorial
Drive, you may wish to visit two nearby sites
on Capitol Avenue. Cross Memorial Drive on
Capitol Avenue. Immediately on the left (east)
on Capitol Avenue is a cubical building made
of Georgia marble. It is the state archives
building which is open to visitors. Approximately 0.5 miles ahead on the right (west)
and after Capitol Avenue crosses Interstate
Highway 20 is the Atlanta-Fulton County
Stadium. The monuments to baseball greats Ty
Cobb and Hank Aaron are located at the
stadium's Capitol Avenue gate. Return to
Memorial Drive.

7 *(0.5) (0.8)*

Go east on Memorial Drive. Proceed with caution. Remember that Memorial Drive is a
heavily-used road. Many spur railroad tracks
serving old industrial sites cross it. And it
passes through a residential area which has
experienced a great deal of change in the past
twenty-five years. Observe the numerous historical markers posted along the next several
miles of the route. These markers pertain to
the Battle of Atlanta action depicted in the
Cyclorama at Grant Park.

8 *(0.6) (1.0)*

The Civil War era Oakland Cemetery is on the
left.

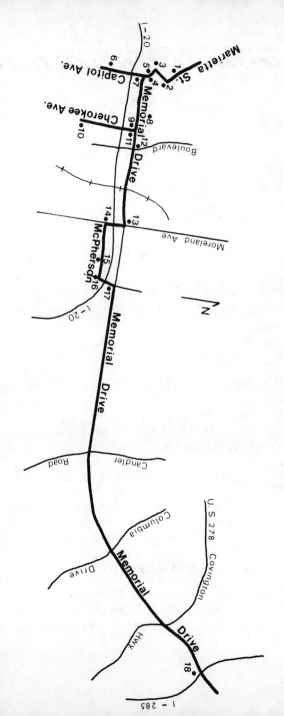

9 *(0.2) (0.3)*

Turn right on to Cherokee Avenue.

10 *(0.5) (0.8)*

Approximately 0.5 mile ahead and on the left in Grant Park is the Cyclorama of the Battle of Atlanta. The newly-renovated Zoo Atlanta is also located in Grant Park.

11 *(0.5) (0.8)*

Return to Memorial Drive and continue eastward.

12 *(0.3) (0.5)*

Boulevard crosses Memorial Drive. Note that the Martin Luther King, Jr. National Historic Site is located approximately 0.6 mile to the north along Boulevard. Continue east along Memorial Drive.

13 *(1.1) (1.8)*

Moreland Avenue is the boundary between Fulton County and DeKalb County. The Little Five Points shopping and entertainment area is located approximately 1.2 miles to the north along Moreland Avenue.

Turn right (south) on to Moreland Avenue. The historical markers "Site of the Battle of Atlanta" and "Legget's Hill" are located on

the left before the bridge over Interstate Highway 20. Cross over I-20.

14 *(0.3) (0.5)*

Turn left (east) on to Flat Shoals Avenue. Where Flat Shoals Avenue bends to the right (southeast), bear to the left (due east) on to McPherson Avenue.

15 *(0.5) (0.8)*

The McPherson Memorial is located on the right (south) at Monument Avenue. Two historical markers are located on the site: "Death of McPherson" and "Historic Ground - 1864."

16 *(0.3) (0.5)*

Turn left (north) on to Maynard Terrace.

17 *(0.3) (0.5)*

Turn right (east) on to Memorial Drive (Ga. 154). Exercise caution in this area.

18 *(6.1) (9.8)*

Memorial Drive crosses over Interstate Highway 285. Be alert to views of Stone Mountain which is located to the east.

Map 2·1·4

1 *(4.3 miles) (6.9 kilometers)*

Bear to the right to remain on Memorial Drive. Follow signs to the Stone Mountain Park West Gate.

2 *(0.6) (1.0)*

At the intersection of Memorial Drive and Main Street, there is a Civil War cemetery on the left. The historical marker "Unknown Confederate Dead" is located at the entrance to the cemetery. Continue on Memorial Drive across Main Street to the West Gate entrance to Stone Mountain Park.

3 *(0.6) (1.0)*

Enter the West Gate to Stone Mountain Park. Bicyclers are usually admitted to the park free of charge. The ticket officer at the gate will give you all the information about the park that you will need, including a map. If you plan to continue on Part 3 of the route, be sure to get directions to the gate next to the Golf Course Club House. It is usually locked and closed to traffic, but you can get someone to let you through with your bicycle. This gate exits onto Bermuda Road.

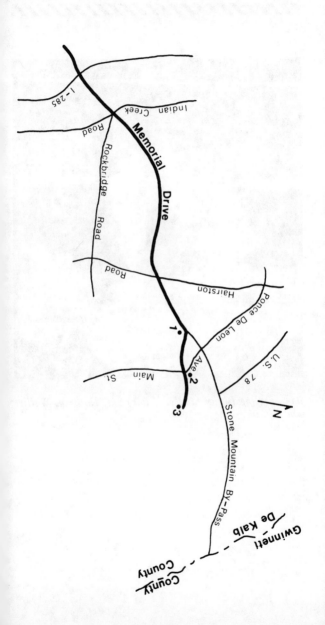

The bicycling Bailey family: (l to r) Sue, Kathryn, Willie, and Ellaine.

PART

3

The March to the Sea

Stone Mountain State Park to Savannah

(Approximately 325 Miles)

After destroying Atlanta, Sherman began the infamous March to the Sea in November 1864. No longer able to supply his troops by rail, Sherman reduced the size of his army to 60,000 men and ordered them to "live off the land" and the supplies they could carry with them, including over 10,000 head of cattle, as they marched eastward across the state. The Union army met little Confederate resistance on this march. General Hood had led the remnants of his army in the opposite direction toward Alabama, leaving Georgia defenseless against the invading army. The vast destruction associated with the march was perpetrated not by battlefield action, but by the looting, scavenging, and trampling of civilian property by the Union troops as they cut a sixty-mile wide path to the Georgia coast. The bicycle route generally traces the course of Sherman's northern flank.

From Stone Mountain to Sandersville, the route crosses the moderate to gently rolling hills of the Georgia Piedmont. The varied rural landscape in this region includes remnants of an extensive cotton culture which once dominated it. Relics include eroded soil, abandoned and recycled cotton warehouses and gin buildings, and sharecropper shacks. The contemporary rural landscape is characterized by pastures, livestock, feed corn, soybeans, some cotton, and much idle cropland. The terrain and rural scenery produce excellent biking conditions.

This section of the route connects a number of interesting places where the local people welcome and expect visiting cyclers. A few miles from Stone Mountain is the village of Walnut Grove. The volunteer fire station there contains a series of paintings depicting the appearance of the village around 1915 when it served a thriving agricultural community. In the village of Jersey, a dentist's office occupies the building constructed in 1930 for the Bank of Jersey which closed in 1933. Next door is Wrens General Store where owner Gertie Wrens markets a great variety of goods and renders good old-fashioned southern hospitality. The ride into Social Circle corresponds to the historic Hightower Trail, a

centuries-old trade route established by
Indians. Marking the center of Social Circle's
round city limit boundary is the town well.
This phenomenon is characteristic of many
small and so-called "roundtowns." The short
distance from Social Circle to Hard Labor
Creek State Park in Rutledge is picturesque.
From Rutledge, the ten-mile strip to Madison
is almost flat. While offering pleasant riding
conditions, this stretch of the route yields a
lesson in rural sociology and agricultural economics. It passes soybean fields where cotton
once was king. Riders can see both relics and
viable remnants of the former cotton culture.
Peach orchards line both sides of some stretches
of this road. Damaged stands of these fruit
trees illustrate the risks posed to farmers by
the vagaries of weather. Cropland idled by the
agricultural implosion in this country and the
close proximity of rural prosperity and poverty
reflect some disturbing economic realities of
rural life in Georgia.

Sherman spared the antebellum houses in
Madison, and the city has capitalized on that
decision. Madison was considered to be the
"most aristocratic town on the stage coach
route from Charleston to New Orleans" before
the Civil War. Over thirty-five restored and
authentically furnished antebellum houses,
churches, and other buildings comprise the
Madison historic district. These structures,
with their beautifully landscaped lawns and
gardens, are open for tours.

The route follows a back road south from
Madison, passes several antebellum plantation
houses, and joins U.S. Highway 441. Although it has a considerable volume of traffic,
U.S. 441 has a wide paved shoulder suitable
for bikers. At Rock Eagle, the world's largest
4-H Center, a granite observation tower over-
looks a large quartz eagle constructed by a prehistoric Indian culture. Eatonton was the
birthplace of Joel Chandler Harris, author of
the "Uncle Remus" stories. A statue of
Harris's Brer Rabbit adorns the Putnam
County Courthouse grounds there. Across the
street, Connelley's Drug Store serves excellent
ice cream dishes and fountain drinks. The Uncle Remus Museum is located a few blocks to
the south. From Eatonton, the route continues along Highway 441 across Lake Sinclair
to Milledgeville.

Sherman instructed the three corps of his army
to converge at a road junction near Milledgeville, Georgia's Civil War capital. The bicycle
route passes the exact place where the army
regrouped. It then leads into the city.
Sherman's army met no resistance there, but
they left a legacy of hate with their actions.
For example, horses were stabled in the St.
Stephens's Episcopal Church, which is still in
use and is located on the former Statehouse
Square. One story holds that Sherman's troops
poured molasses in the church's organ pipes.
Today, Georgia Military College occupies the
old state capital complex. The Old Governor's
Mansion on the campus of Georgia College

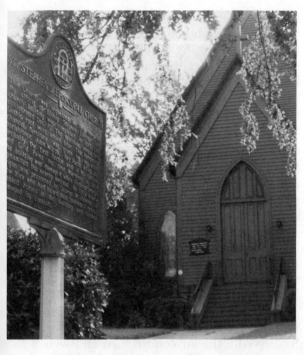

St. Stephen's Church, Milledgeville, Ga.

currently serves as both a museum open to visitors and the home of the college president. Another interesting place in Milledgeville is the site of Georgia's former state mental hospital. Much pioneering research and treatment of mental illness in this country was conducted there. In recent years, some parts of the facility have been converted to house prisoners.

The route from Milledgeville to Sandersville is quite hilly. Between the village of Deepstep and Sandersville the route passes a number of active kaolin mining and processing operations. Kaolin, a type of clay, is Georgia's leading economic mineral. The pervasive effect of kaolin on the region is reflected by the name of Sandersville's primary shopping center, Kaolin Plaza. The Clean Hangout is a combination gameroom and coin laundry located there. On typically hot and humid summer days in Sandersville the air conditioned and well-managed Clean Hangout is a refreshing refuge where bikers can do their laundry.

Beyond Sandersville, the route becomes appreciably flatter as it enters the Coastal Plain region. At Davisboro, the owner of Posser's Store cheerfully relates the history of that place, including a visit by Sherman, and will discuss contemporary issues. The antique bottle collection which he displays in the store and the artesian well behind the building are also attractions of this village. Irrigated soybean fields line the road into Louisville and

represent Georgia's most valuable agricultural product.

Louisville was Georgia's first inland capital. Several sites of interest to visit there include a Revolutionary War era cemetery, a slave marketplace, and the county courthouse where a monument proclaims this as the place where the Yazoo land fraud papers were destroyed with "fire drawn from heaven." About fifteen miles south of Louisville along the Ogeechee River the route passes Old Town Plantation, established in 1767. It is the oldest continuously operated plantation in the state. The family which owns and operates it welcomes visitors. They tell about a photograph that exists of author Joel Chandler Harris sitting on the front porch of the old homeplace and contend that Old Town may have influenced some of Harris's "Uncle Remus" tales.

Sherman's strategy was to follow the course of the Ogeechee River from Louisville to the coast. From Old Town, the route proceeds through the towns of Midville and Millen toward the city of Statesboro. Located a few miles north of Millen is Magnolia Springs State Park. The Confederate army built a prison on that site to house inmates transferred from Andersonville as Sherman threatened the state. The Confederates believed that one of Sherman's goals in Georgia was to liberate the Union prisoners at Andersonville. South of Millen at the tiny hamlet of Scarboro on the bank of the Ogeechee River, the pure and icy water of a powerful artesian well blasts through a pipe to the surface. This refreshing spot is a favorite for local fishermen who have easy boating access to the river and for others, including bikers, who wish to soak in the well water. The route from Scarboro to the outskirts of Statesboro passes through a beautiful agricultural area.

Flat terrain dominates the bicycle route from Statesboro to the coast. Pine forests, broken primarily by tobacco and soybean fields, dominate the landscape. Near the small town of Stilson a broad and shallow place along the Ogeechee River invites wading, swimming, and skipping rocks. Tom Sawyer and Huck Finn would have loved it.

Before Sherman could attack his objective at Savannah, he had to resupply his army. The Confederate Fort MacAllister guarded the mouth of the Ogeechee River and prevented a Union fleet from reaching Sherman's army, camped ten miles upstream at King's Bridge. On December 13, 1864, one of Sherman's divisions overwhelmed the small Confederate garrison and captured the fort during a fifteen minute ground attack. With the fort's guns silenced, the Union ships moved upstream to King's Bridge to distribute supplies, including siege material, to Sherman's troops. When news of Fort MacAllister's capture and Sherman's preparation for a siege reached Savannah, the Confederates hastily abandoned the city. Sherman marched unopposed into the city on

Christmas day and promptly wired the news to President Lincoln as a Christmas gift.

The bicycle route leads to King's Bridge and to the Fort MacAllister State Historic Site in Richmond Hill State Park. The park has a museum and provides guided tours of the fort. When our student groups visit there, the park superintendent allows them to camp on the same ground where Sherman's troops slept. He also gives them an elaborate tour of the fort complete with demonstrations by uniformed soldiers.

The bicycle route ends at the Savannah Visitor Center located about twenty miles from Fort MacAllister. The Center provides guidance for touring Georgia's premier city. Restoration of the 250-year-old city has been in progress for over twenty years. The scenic Savannah National Historic Landmark District contains the cobblestone streets, shaded squares, mansions, and cottages which characterized the original city plan. A visit to the Green-Meldrim House where Sherman headquartered while in Savannah completes our tour route.

Directions:

PART 3 · SEGMENT 1

Stone Mountain State Park to Hard Labor Creek State Park

Length

Approximately 39 miles (50 kilometers)

Terrain

This part of the route is in the Piedmont land-surface region. The terrain is hilly between Stone Mountain and Centerville but becomes more gently rolling from there to Hard Labor Creek.

Road Surface

The roads are in good condition. Most are smooth asphalt, but several stretches have coarse textured pavement. Throughout Georgia, road shoulders are inconsistent and hazardous.

Traffic

Traffic is generally heavy in the suburban area around Stone Mountain, especially along Rockbridge Rd. where bikers must exercise caution. From Centerville, however, rural settlement landscape and light traffic characterize the route.

Hazards

Extreme caution is necessary in several places. Rockbridge Rd. is narrow and has relatively heavy traffic. Cross Ga. Hwy. 124 carefully at Centerville. You may encounter fast-moving vehicles along Ga. Hwy. 20. In Walnut Grove, Ga. Hwy. 81 has relatively heavy traffic, especially at the intersection with Ga. Hwy. 138. The turn from Hwy. 81 onto the Walnut Grove-Jersey Rd. (James Odum Rd.) is at the top of a hill, and oncoming traffic may be hard to judge.

Accommodations

Stone Mountain State Park offers both camping and a motel, and there are many motels near the park. Hard Labor Creek State Park has camping and cabins. Call in advance for cabin reservations. The nearest motels to this park are at Madison. Many stores are located along this segment. Walnut Grove, Jersey, and Social Circle provide a variety of services.

Population of Central Places

Stone Mountain - 4,867, Walnut Grove - 387, Jersey - 201, Social Circle - 2,591.

Map 3·1·1

1 *(0.0 miles) (0.0 kilometers)*

Bicycles are prohibited on U.S. 78 at the Stone Mountain Park East Gate. You must, therefore, use the gate adjacent to the Stone Mountain Park Golf Clubhouse. This gate is usually locked, but park security officers or clubhouse personnel will open it for you. From the gate go straight ahead (east) on Bermuda Road.

2 *(0.6) (1.0)*

At the stop sign turn right on to West Park Place.

3 *(1.0) (1.6)*

At the stop sign turn right (south) on to Rockbridge Road. This narrow road often has heavy traffic.

4 *(1.0) (1.6)*

Bear left (east) on to Annistown Road. Traffic will decrease from this point, but there are some steep hills ahead.

5 *(3.3) (5.3)*

Annistown Rd. ends at Ga. 124 in Centerville. Cross Ga. 124 and continue eastward on

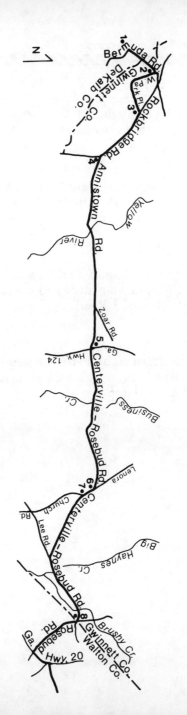

the Centerville-Rosebud Road. Stop and look
back occasionally for views of Stone Mountain.

6 *(2.4) (3.9)*

At the stop sign turn right. Lenora Church
Road and Centerville-Rosebud Road run together for a short distance.

7 *(0.2) (0.3)*

Bear left at the Lenora Church (which will be
on the right after you turn) and continue on
Centerville-Rosebud Road.

8 *(2.4) (3.9)*

In Rosebud, turn right at the stop sign on the
Rosebud Road. Note the rock structure on
the right at this stop sign.

Map 3·1·2

1 *(1.0 miles) (1.6 kilometers)*

At the stop sign turn left on to Ga. 20.

2 *(0.4) (0.6)*

At the Center Hill Church, turn right on to Center Hill Church Road.

3 *(4.2) (6.7)*

Turn right on to Emmett Still Road. Take care not to miss this turn. For whatever reason, it is the one which riders in our groups miss most frequently.

4 *(2.6) (4.2)*

Continue on Emmett Still Road from the point at which Guthrie Road meets it from the right and Cemetery Road bears to the left. Walnut Grove Park is ahead on the left.

5 *(0.6) (1.0)*

At the stop sign, turn right (south) on to Ga. 81.

6 *(0.3) (0.5)*

At the intersection of Ga. 81 and Ga. 138 in Walnut Grove, the City Hall and Volunteer Fire Station is on the right. Inside this

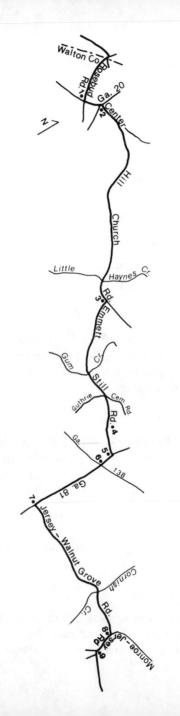

building is a series of paintings which depict scenes in Walnut Grove when it was a thriving agricultural service center. Bicyclers are warmly welcomed at this place. Continue south along Ga. 81.

7 *(1.6) (2.6)*

Turn left (east) on to the Jersey-Walnut Grove Road (also called the James Odum Road). Exercise caution at this turn. It is at the top of a small hill, and the view of approaching traffic is poor.

8 *(3.1) (5.0)*

Turn right (south) on to the Monroe-Jersey Road. The town center of Jersey is a short distance ahead. Make a stop at Wrens Store and talk to Gertie Wrens.

9 *(0.5) (0.8)*

Turn left (east) on to the Jersey-Social Circle Road.

Map 3·1·3

1 *(6.7 miles) (10.8 kilometers)*

In Social Circle, at the red light, the Jersey-Social Circle Road crosses Ga. 11. On the right is the federal historical marker "The Hightower Trail." The town well, the center of the circular city limits of Social Circle, is to the right of center in this intersection. Continue across Ga. 11 along the Jersey-Social Circle Road.

2 *(0.4) (0.6)*

Cross the relatively new bridge over the railroad, turn right, and cross another bridge over the railroad. At the stop sign beyond the second bridge turn left (east) on to Ga. 229. The Georgia Railroad parallels Ga. 229 on the left (north).

3 *(1.6) (2.6)*

At the sign "Hard Labor Creek State Park 5" turn left on to Knox Chapel Road. Cross the railroad and proceed to the park.

4 *(5.0) (8.0)*

This segment ends at the Hard Labor Creek State Park Headquarters.

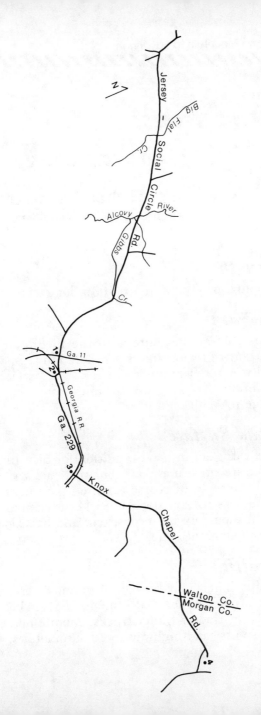

N

Jersey – Social Circle

Big Flat Cr.

Alcovy River

Gibbs Rd.

Cr.

1. Ga 11

2.

Georgia R R

Ga. 229

3. Knox

Chapel

Walton Co.
Morgan Co.

Rd.

4.

Directions:

PART 3 · SEGMENT 2

Hard Labor Creek State Park to Milledgeville

Length

Approximately 62 miles (100 kilometers)

Terrain

This part of the route is in the Piedmont landsurface region and is generally hilly, especially at the beginning and end. The surface is almost flat along the 10 miles from Rutledge to Madison.

Road Surface

The roads are in good condition for bicycling. Most are smooth asphalt, but there are several stretches of coarse textured pavement. Road construction along U.S. 441 is common. Road shoulders are inconsistent and hazardous throughout the state.

Traffic

Traffic is generally busy in Madison, Eatonton, and Milledgeville. Traffic along U.S. 441 includes tractor-trailer trucks, mobile home transports, and highway-speed automobiles.

Hazards

Use extreme caution in the towns of Madison, Eatonton, and Milledgeville, all along U.S. 441, and at Lake Sinclair, where vehicles towing boats are common. Eatonton is a mobile home manufacturing center. Road construction on U.S. 441 poses hazards to bicyclers.

Accommodations

There are excellent camping facilities at Hard Labor Creek State Park, Rock Eagle 4H Center near Eatonton, and Lake Sinclair located north of Milledgeville. Motel accommodations are numerous in Madison, Eatonton, and Milledgeville. Each town offers a wide variety of services, and there are stores located along the rural stretches of the route.

Population of Central Places

Rutledge - 694, Madison - 2,954, Eatonton - 4,833, and Milledgeville - 12,176.

Map 3·2·1

1 *(0.0 miles) (0.0 kilometers)*

From the Trading Post at the Hard Labor Creek State Park Headquarters, turn left on to Knox Chapel Road.

2 *(0.5) (0.8)*

At the stop sign, turn right (south) on to Fairplay Road and proceed to Rutledge.

3 *(2.8) (4.5)*

In Rutledge cross the railroad, turn left (east) on to Dixie Highway, and proceed to Madison. In Rutledge, note that the old railroad depot has been converted to the City Hall.

4 *(8.1) (13.0)*

On the right, look for the almost-hidden stone marker commemorating the location of a tavern and rest stop on the stagecoach line from Charleston to New Orleans. Madison was considered "the most aristocratic town on the line."

5 *(0.1) (0.2)*

At the railroad, turn left to visit a major peach packing plant. It is a short venture that, in

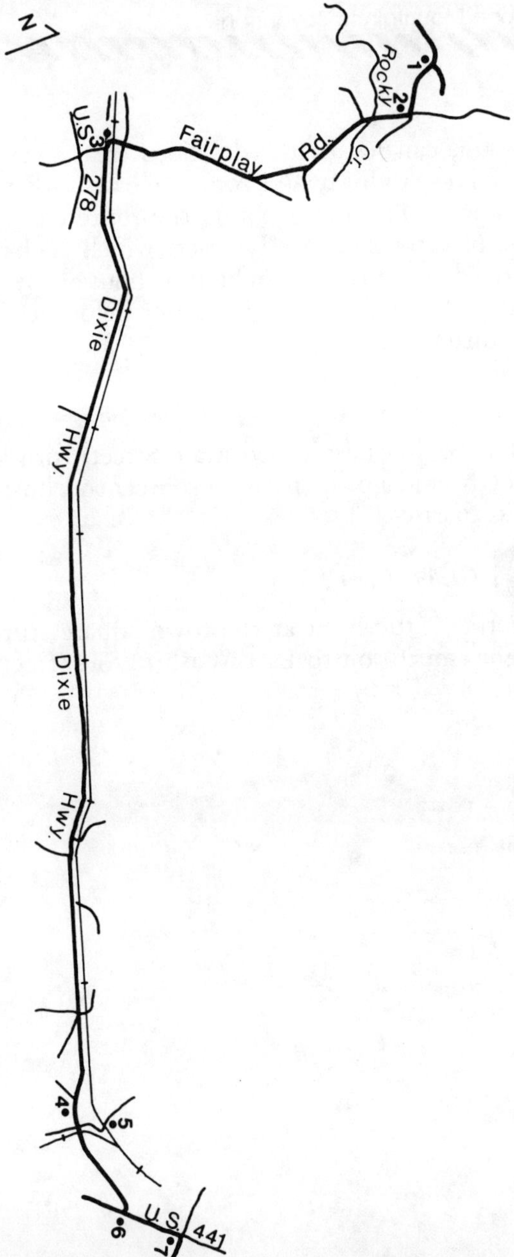

N
1
2
Rocky Cr.
Fairplay Rd.
U.S. 278
3
Dixie Hwy.
Dixie Hwy.
4
5
6
U.S. 441
7

season, can result in a delicious treat. Return to Dixie Highway and continue eastward into Madison. From this point, the route enters the Madison Historic District, which is characterized by restored antebellum houses. Be sure to tour the historic district before leaving Madison.

6 *(0.8) (1.3)*

At U.S. 441 (also called Main Street) turn left (north) and go to the Madison central business district.

7 *(0.5) (0.8)*

At the traffic light at the town square, turn right (south) on to East Washington Street.

Madison, Ga.

Map 3·2·2

1 *(1.4 miles) (3.2 kilometers)*

At the Madison city limit sign, East Washington Street becomes Bethany Road. Continue southward along Bethany Road.

2 *(3.5) (5.6)*

An antebellum house is located on the left.

3 *(1.3) (2.7)*

Bear to the right at Bethany Church and remain on Bethany Road.

4 *(2.3) (3.7)*

Turn right (west) on to Seven Island Road.

5 *(1.2) (1.9)*

Turn left (south) on to U.S. 441. Joe's Store is located at this intersection. Exercise caution on U.S. 441. It has a paved and marked shoulder suitable for a bicycle.

6 *(2.8) (4.5)*

Leave Morgan County and enter Putnam County.

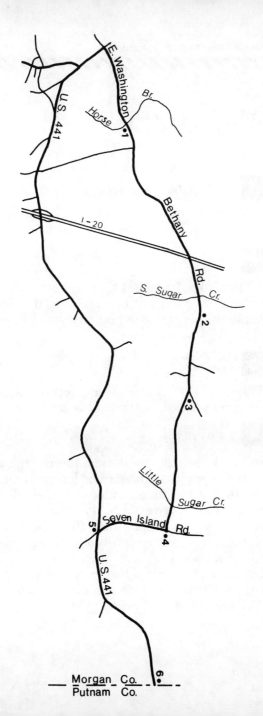

Map 3·2·3

1 *(3.0 miles) (4.8 kilometers)*

The historic Tompkins Inn, a nineteenth century roadhouse, is located on the left.

2 *(1.3) (2.1)*

At the Rock Eagle 4H Center, turn right at this entrance to the center and visit the Rock Eagle effigy constructed by prehistoric indians. Signs lead to the effigy.

3 *(1.0) (1.6)*

From the Rock Eagle effigy, return to U.S. 441 and proceed southward toward Eatonton.

4 *(6.9) (11.1)*

In Eatonton, take some time to visit the Putnam County Courthouse and grounds where the Brer Rabbit statue is located. Connolley's Drug Store is across U.S. 441 from the courthouse and has a soda fountain. The Uncle Remus Museum is two blocks south of the courthouse on U.S. 441. There are many antebellum and victorian houses in the vicinity of the courthouse. Continue southward on U.S. 441 toward Milledgeville.

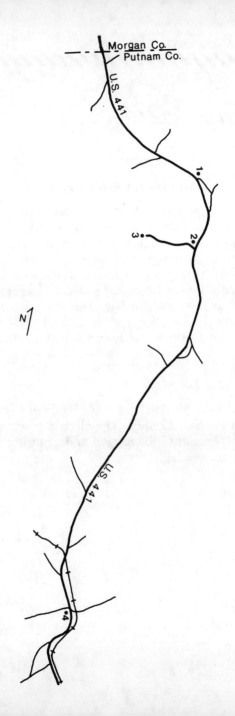

Map 3·2·4

1 *(2.2 miles) (3.5 kilometers)*

At the junction of U.S. 441 and U.S. 129, bear left and continue southward on U.S. 441. This can be a dangerous junction for bicyclers. Exercise caution as you travel through it. Beyond this point, the smokestacks on the Georgia Power Company's electric generating plant at the Lake Sinclair Dam may be seen to the south. It is located on U.S. 441 at the Puntam County-Baldwin County boundary line.

2 *(10.2) (16.4)*

Cross Lake Sinclair and enter Baldwin County from Putnam County. The electric power plant is on the right. Recreation and camping facilities are available here.

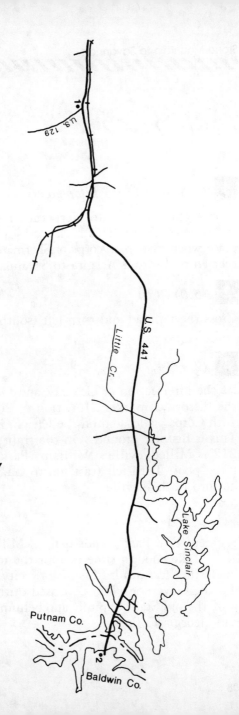

Map 3·2·5

1 *(1.6 miles) (2.6 kilometers)*

Turn right (west) on to Meriweather Road at the large cemetery. This back road leads to the place where the three corps of Sherman's army met en route from Atlanta to Savannah.

2 *(5.0) (8.0)*

Cross the railroad and turn left (south) on to Ga. 212.

3 *(2.9) (4.7)*

At the intersection of Ga. 212 and Ga. 22, the historical marker "Junction of 20th and 14th Corps" is located on the left of Ga. 212. This is historic ground. On the right of Ga. 212 is Milledgeville's Williams Park swimming pool. Turn left (east) on to Ga. 22 and go into Milledgeville.

4 *(3.5) (5.6)*

Segment 2 of Part 3 ends here in Milledgeville. Take enough time to tour the many interesting features in this historic city, including the Governor's Mansion used during the war, the old State Capitol, antebellum houses, and Georgia College.

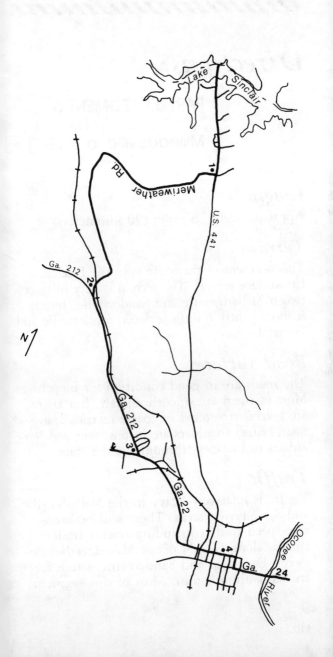

/////////////////////////////

Directions:

PART 3 · SEGMENT 3

Milledgeville to Louisville

Length
Approximately 56 miles (90 kilometers)

Terrain
This segment of the route is in the Piedmont landsurface region. The terrain is very hilly between Milledgeville and Sandersville, but it is more gently rolling between Sandersville and Louisville.

Road Surface
The roads are in good condition for bicycling. Most of them are smooth asphalt, but there are several strectches of coarse textured pavement. Road shoulders are inconsistent and hazardous to bicyclers throughout the state.

Traffic
Traffic is relatively heavy in the Milledgeville and Sandersville areas. There will be highway-speed traffic, including tractor trailer trucks, along Ga. 24 out of Milledgeville. Between Deepstep and Sandersville watch for trucks hauling kaolin. Most of this segment,

however, traverses a lightly travelled rural landscape.

Hazards

Exercise caution in the town traffic in Milledgeville, Sandersville, and Louisville. Traffic along Ga. 24 is fast moving and includes tractor trailer trucks. Watch for kaolin trucks between Deepstep and Sandersville.

Accommodations

Camping and motels are available between Lake Sinclair and downtown Milledgeville. Camping permission is available at the Lions Club Park in Louisville. Milledgeville, Sandersville, and (to a lesser extent) Louisville have a variety of services. Deepstep has a general store. Posser's general store in Davisboro is a treat to visit. There are no stores between Ga. 24 and Deepstep and between Deepstep and Sandersville.

Population of Central Places

Milledgeville - 12,176, Deepstep - 120, Sandersville - 6,137, Davisboro - 433, and Louisville - 2,823.

Map 3·3·1

1 *(0.0 miles) (0.0 kilometers)*

Go east on Ga. 24 (also Ga. 22) across the Oconee River Bridge.

2 *(0.3) (0.5)*

Posted on the right are three historical markers: "Old Fort Fidius (1793-1797)," "The Rock Landing," and "Campsite of Union Army."

3 *(3.4) (5.5)*

Bear to the right (east) to remain on Ga. 24.

4 *(3.4) (5.5)*

Turn left (east) on to Deepstep Road. Sometimes the sign for this road may not be posted, and this turn is easy to miss.

5 *(1.4) (2.3)*

Located on the left is the nineteenth century O'Quinn's Mill.

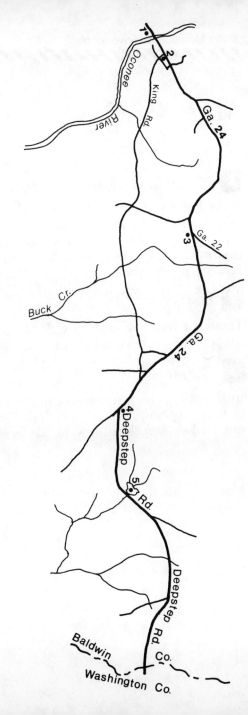

Map 3·3·2

1 *(3.1 miles) (5.0 kilometers)*

Leave Baldwin County and enter Washington County. Note the active, abandoned, and reclaimed kaolin mines from this point in Washington County. There are a few short and very steep hills ahead.

2 *(5.4) (8.7)*

There is a relatively elaborate flea market on the left at a place called Goattown.

3 *(0.2) (0.3)*

In Deepstep, the management of the general store is very hospitable to bicyclers. Continue east on Deepstep Road toward Sandersville.

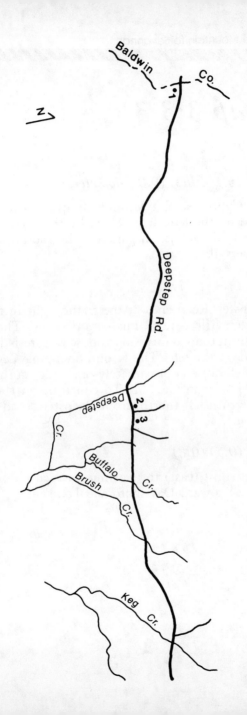

Map 3·3·3

1 *(6.1 miles) (9.8 kilometers)*

The Cyprus Kaolin Mining Company is located on the left. It is served by the Sandersville Railroad which parallels the route into Sandersville.

2 *(4.4) (7.1)*

Deepstep Road ends at the traffic light in the Sandersville central business district. The Washington County Courthouse Square is located on the left. The Kaolin Shopping Center is located approximately one mile south of this point on Ga. 24. To continue on the route turn left (north) from Deepstep Road on to Ga. 24.

3 *(0.5) (0.8)*

Turn right (east) to continue eastward along Ga. 24 toward Davisboro and Louisville.

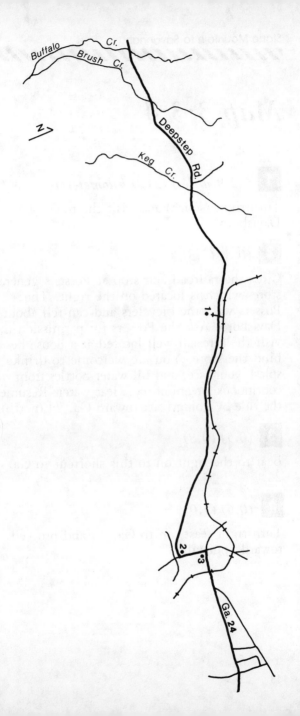

Map 3·3·4

1 *(12.9 miles) (21.0 kilometers)*

Turn right (south) and visit the town of Davisboro.

2 *(0.8) (1.3)*

Cross the railroad and stop at Posser's general store, which is located on the right. The Possers welcome bicyclers and can tell about Davisboro. Ask the Possers for permission to visit the artesian well located at a house behind the store. You are welcome to drink, splash your face, and fill water bottles from the continuous stream of icy, clear water. Resume the ride by going back toward Ga. 24 (north).

3 *(0.5) (0.8)*

Bear to the right on to this shortcut to Ga. 24.

4 *(0.6) (1.0)*

Turn right (east) on to Ga. 24 and proceed toward Louisville.

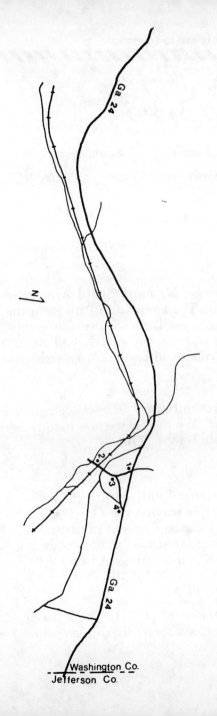

N

Ga 24

Ga 24

Washington Co.
Jefferson Co.

Map 3·3·5

1 *(3.2 miles) (5.1 kilometers)*

Leave Washington County and enter Jefferson County.

2 *(6.9) (11.1)*

Cross the Ogeechee River.

3 *(0.7) (1.1)*

The Georgia National Guard Armory is on the right. The Lions Club Park is on the left. Camping is available with special permission at either of these two places. Call the mayor of Louisville in advance to make arrangements.

4 *(1.7) (2.7)*

A pre-Revolutionary War era cemetery is on the right. Try to find a grave marker bearing a date before 1776.

5 *(0.2) (0.3)*

At the traffic light, turn right on to West Broad Street to visit the Old Market House and the Jefferson County Courthouse. Historical markers are posted at both places. Return to Ga. 24 and continue eastward.

6 *(1.0) (1.6)*

Turn right on to U.S. 1. The Louisville Motor Lodge is a short distance ahead on the right.

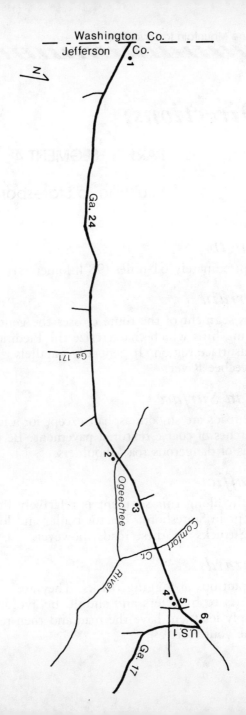

Directions:

PART 3 · SEGMENT 4

Louisville to Statesboro

Length

Approximately 61 miles (98 kilometers)

Terrain

This segment of the route crosses the gently rolling hills which characterize the Piedmont landsurface region. It generally parallels the Ogeechee River.

Road Surface

The roads are smooth asphalt except for a few stretches of coarse textured pavement. Be cautious of dangerous road shoulders.

Traffic

Traffic along this segment is relatively light except in Statesboro. Tractor trailer and logging trucks use these roads, however.

Hazards

Be cautious of logging trucks. They are threats to bicyclers and should be avoided. Simply let them have the road and then resume your ride.

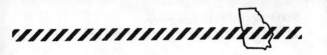

Accommodations

With permission, camping is available in Louisville at the National Guard Armory and the Lions Club Park. These facilities are located opposite one another approximately one mile west of Louisville on Ga. 24. We recommend the Louisville Motor Lodge on U.S. 1, if you are not camping. Statesboro has many motels, and camping is available at private campgrounds there. The towns along this segment provide a variety of services. Statesboro has a bicycle shop.

Population of Central Places

Louisville - 2,823, Midville - 670, Millen - 3,988, and Statesboro - 14,866.

Willie Bailey cooling off at Scarboro's artesian well.

123

Map 3·4·1

1 *(1.0 miles) (1.6 kilometers)*

From the intersection of Ga. 24 and U.S. 1, go one mile to the caution light and turn left (east) on to Ga. 17.

2 *(7.9) (12.7)*

Old Town Plantation is located on the left. A historical marker is posted in front of this colonial era settlement. Visitors are usually welcome.

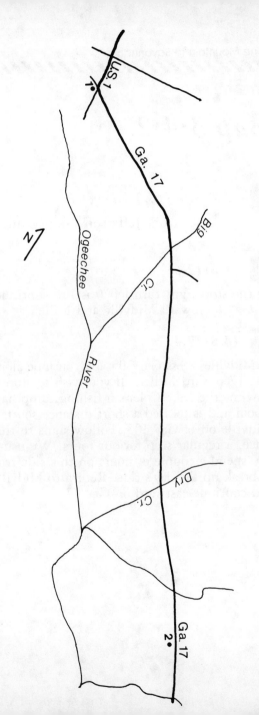

Map 3·4·2

1 *(2.7 miles) (4.3 kilometers)*

Ga. 17 passes from Jefferson County into Burke County.

2 *(1.6) (2.6)*

At the stop sign, turn left (east) to continue on Ga. 17 toward Midville and Millen.

3 *(4.6) (7.4)*

In Midville, cross Ga. 305 and continue along Ga. 17 toward Millen. If you wish to stop for a swim, the Lake Coleman fishing camp has a pool and is located a short distance south of Midville off of Ga. 305. Follow signs to this place, a regular stop for our tours. We usually spend a couple of hours on this side trip to break up the day's ride. Return to Midville, and continue eastward on Ga. 17.

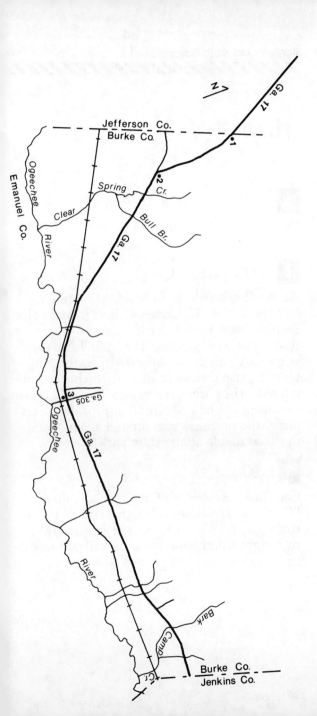

Map 3·4·3

1 *(5.5 miles) (8.8 kilometers)*

Ga. 17 passes from Burke County into Jenkins County.

2 *(11.6) (18.7)*

At the first traffic light inside the Millen city limit, Ga. 17 crosses U.S. 25. Magnolia Springs State Park is located several miles to the left (north) along U.S. 25. It was the site of a Confederate-operated prison camp. Union prisoners were moved to this hastily erected prison from Andersonville, as Sherman advanced. When Sherman approached this place, the prisoners were moved again. Camping is available at the state park.

3 *(0.8) (1.3)*

Continue eastward on Ga. 17 (also called Winthrope Avenue) through Millen. Follow the signs for Ga. 17. At the traffic light, turn right (south) and cross the railroad to continue to Ga. 17.

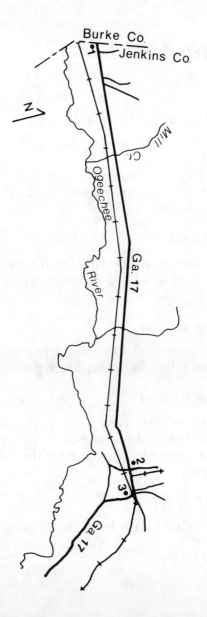

Map 3·4·4

1 *(7.2 miles) (11.6 kilometers)*

At Scarboro, turn right at the church and ride down to the Ogeechee River, where the road ends. To the left there is a powerful artesian well; do not miss it. Return to Ga. 17 and proceed south.

2 *(3.6) (5.8)*

At the sign to Rocky Ford, turn right on to Rocky Ford Road and proceed into the town of Rocky Ford.

3 *(2.4) (3.9)*

After crossing the Ogeechee River in Rocky Ford, turn left on to Old River Road.

4 *(4.9) (7.9)*

At the stop sign, turn right on to Lakeview Road and proceed toward Statesboro. Lakeview Road becomes Main Street inside the Statesboro city limit.

5 *(7.0) (11.3)*

At the railroad, bear left on to Fair Street (also Ga. 67). The Statesboro Recreation Center is located on the left.

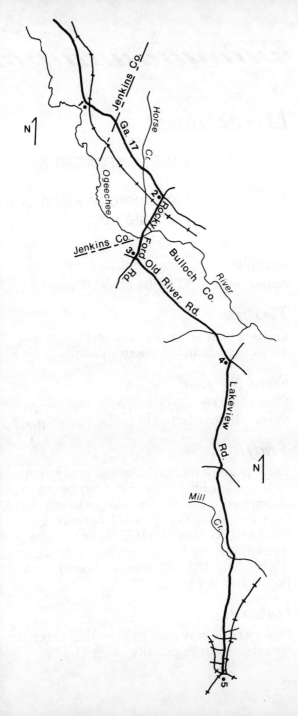

Directions:

PART 3 · SEGMENT 5

Statesboro to Richmond Hill State Park

Length

Approximately 72 Miles (116 kilometers)

Terrain

This segment is on the Coastal Plain land-surface region and is relatively flat.

Road Surface

Most roads are smooth asphalt, but there are several short stretches of coarse pavement.

Traffic

There is a mixture of light and heavy traffic on this segment. Heavy traffic can be expected in Statesboro and Pooler, along Quacco Road from Pooler, and on U.S. 17 between Quacco Road and Richmond Hill. Expect highway-speed traffic with tractor trailer and logging trucks along U.S. 80 between Statesboro and Pooler and along U.S. 17.

Hazards

Heavy traffic and road construction make the Statesboro area, especially along U.S. 80,

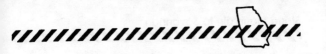

hazardous to bicyclers. U.S. 17 from Quacco Road to Richmond Hill is the most dangerous part of the route. The treacherous road shoulder adds to the danger posed by the high-speed and careless automobile and truck traffic on this stretch of road. **Be careful on U.S. 17.**

Accommodations

Camping is available in Statesboro at private campgrounds. Statesboro has many motels. There are excellent camping facilities at Richmond Hill State Park. Several motels are located in and near the city of Richmond Hill. The towns along this segment, especially Statesboro, offer a variety of services. There is a bicycle shop in Statesboro. Numerous rural stores are scattered along the route.

Population of Central Places

Statesboro - 14,866, Brooklet - 1,035, Pooler - 2,543, Richmond Hill - 1,177, and Savannah - 141,634.

Map 3·5·1

1 *(0.0 miles) (0.0 kilometers)*

From the Statesboro Recreation Center, go north on Zetterower Street.

2 *(0.8) (1.3)*

At the second traffic light, turn right on to Savannah Street.

3 *(0.4) (0.6)*

Turn right (east) on to U.S. 80.

4 *(8.2) (13.2)*

The town of Brooklet is on the right. Continue along U.S. 80.

5 *(8.4) (13.5)*

At the town of Stilson, turn left on to Ga. 119 Connector.

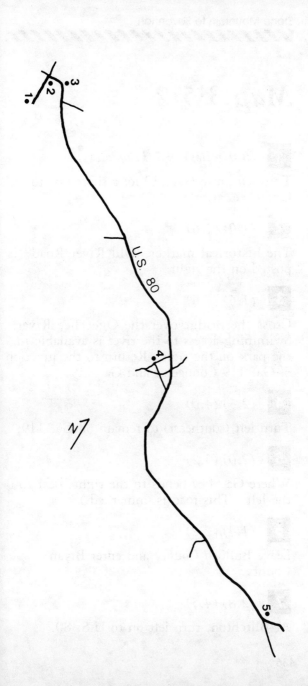

Map 3·5·2

1 *(6.0 miles) (9.7 kilometers)*

Turn left on to Ga. 119 for a short ride to the Ogeechee River.

2 *(1.0) (1.6)*

The historical marker "Old River Road" is posted on the right.

3 *(1.6) (2.6)*

Cross the bridge over the Ogeechee River. Swimming access to the river is available in the park on the right. Return to the junction of Ga. 119 Connector and Ga. 119.

4 *(2.5) (4.0)*

Turn left (southeast) to remain on Ga. 119.

5 *(2.0) (3.2)*

Where Ga. 119 bends to the right, bear to the left. (This road is unmarked.)

6 *(1.4) (2.2)*

Leave Bulloch County and enter Bryan County.

7 *(2.8) (4.5)*

At Blitchton, turn left on to U.S. 80.

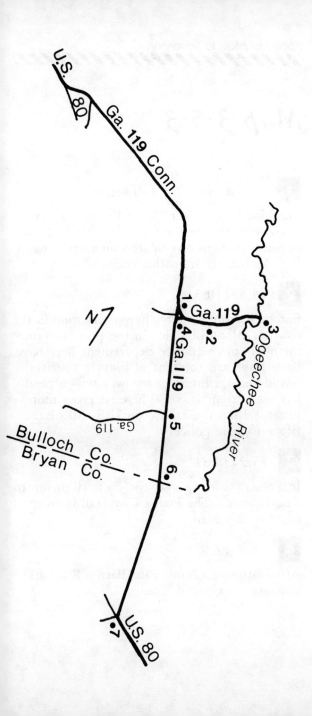

Map 3·5·3

1 *(1.3 miles) (2.1 kilometers)*

The historical marker "Jenks Bridge" is posted at the bridge over the Ogeechee River. Some of Sherman's troops floated on rafts toward Fort McAllister from this site.

2 *(6.5) (10.5)*

Enter Chatham County. Exercise caution in the town of Bloomingdale. In the past, certain members of the police department here have been less than tolerant of bicycle tourists. Avoid the old highway roadway which parallels the current U.S. 80 here. It poses more hazards than the traffic on U.S. 80 or the Bloomingdale police.

3 *(5.2) (8.3)*

In Pooler, turn right at the traffic light on to Rogers Street. The Pooler City Hall is on the right at this turn.

4 *(1.8) (2.9)*

At the stop sign, cross Pine Barren Road and continue on Quacco Road.

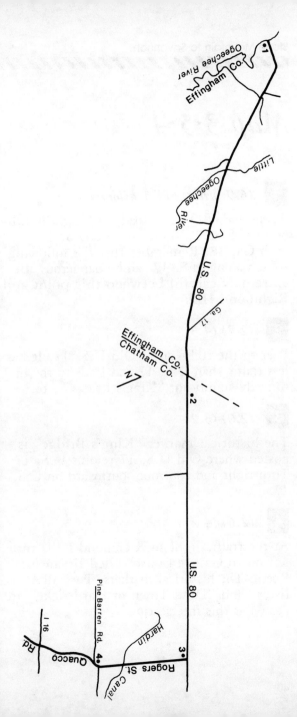

Map 3·5·4

1 *(6.9 miles) (11.1 kilometers)*

At the end of Quacco Road, turn right (south) on to U.S. 17. Do not confuse U.S. 17 with Ga. 17. Remember that the following stretch along U.S. 17 can be dangerous. **Be extremely careful between this point and Richmond Hill.**

2 *(2.7) (4.3)*

Bear to the right on to Old U.S. 17. It has less traffic than U.S. 17 and leads to the historically significant "King's Bridge" site.

3 *(2.0) (3.2)*

The historical marker "King's Bridge" is posted where Old U.S. 17 rejoins U.S. 17. Turn right and continue southward on U.S. 17.

4 *(2.6) (4.2)*

At the traffic light in Richmond Hill, turn left on to Ga. 144 (also called Bryan Neck Road). The historical markers "Fort McAllister" and "Dead Town of Hardwicke" are posted at this intersection.

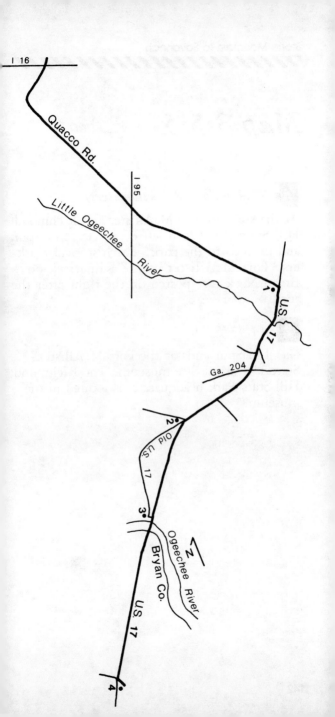

Map 3·5·5

1 *(5.4 miles) (8.7 kilometers)*

At the signs to Fort McAllister and Richmond Hill State Park, turn left on to Ga. 144 Spur and proceed to the park. The historical markers "Fort McAllister" and "Kilpatrick on Bryan Neck" are posted on the right after the turn.

2 *(4.4) (7.1)*

Ga. 144 Spur ends at the Fort McAllister State Historical Site museum. The Richmond Hill State Park headquarters is located in the museum.

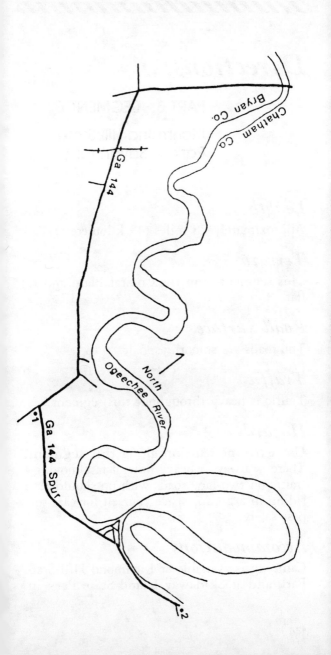

Directions:

PART 3 · SEGMENT 6

Richmond Hill State Park to Savannah

Length

Approximately 28 miles (45 kilometers)

Terrain

This segment is in the Coastal Plain and is flat.

Road Surface

The roads are smooth asphalt.

Traffic

Traffic is heavy throughout this segment.

Hazards

Use extreme caution along this segment. There is always a heavy flow of fast-moving traffic on two-lane roads with no shoulder. If riding in a group, space yourself for cars to pass safely.

Accommodations

Camping is available at Richmond Hill State Park and at Skidaway Island State Park in

Savannah. Several motels are located in the Richmond Hill area, and they abound in Savannah. Savannah is a major city and has several excellent bicycle shops.

Population of Central Places
Richmond Hill - 1,177 and Savannah - 141,634.

Map 3·6·1

1 *(0.0 miles) (0.0 kilometers)*

From Fort McAllister State Historic Site, follow Ga. 144 Spur toward Richmond Hill.

2 *(4.4) (7.1)*

Turn right on to Ga. 144.

3 *(5.4) (8.7)*

At the traffic light in Richmond Hill, turn right (north) on to U.S. 17.

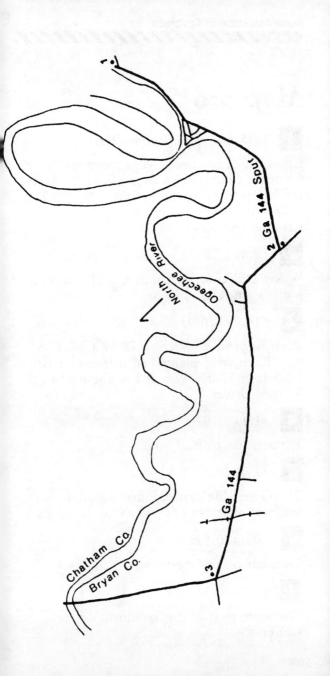

Map 3·6·2

1 *(2.5 miles) (4.0 kilometers)*

Cross the Ogeechee River bridge and enter
Chatham County from Bryan County. Across
the bridge turn left on to Old U.S. 17. The
historical marker "King's Bridge" is on the
left after the turn.

2 *(2.0) (3.2)*

Where Old U.S. 17 rejoins U.S. 17, continue
north along U.S. 17.

3 *(10.2) (16.4)*

Turn right on to Victory Drive (also U.S.
80). Palm trees planted in memory of fallen
soldiers of World War II line the median of
Victory Drive.

4 *(1.1) (1.8)*

Turn left on to Bull Street.

5 *(1.3) (2.1)*

The Green-Meldrim House, located on the
left, was Sherman's Savannah headquarters.

6 *(0.3) (0.5)*

Turn left on to Liberty Street.

7 *(0.3) (0.5)*

The route ends at the Savannah Visitors
Center.

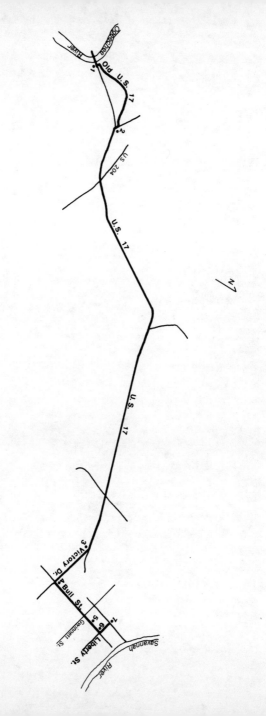

Appendix A:

Rules of the Road

Georgia Bicycle Laws

Every person riding a bicycle upon a road way must obey the same traffic laws governing the drivers of motor vehicles.

1. Obey all signs, signals, and pavement markings.

2. Signal all turns and stops, using the standard hand signals.

3. Ride with traffic on the extreme right side of the road. Do not weave in and out of traffic.

4. Ride no more than two side by side. (It's safest to ride single file.)

5. Always use a bicycle path near the roadway, if one is provided.

6. Never hang on to moving vehicles by any method.

7. Never carry a passenger unless an attached seat is available for the passenger.

8. Every bicycle in use at night time must have a headlight which is visible from at least 300 feet ahead and a red rear reflector which is visible from at least 300 feet to

the rear. In addition to the rear reflector, a red light may be used.

Standards of Safety and Courtesy

Pass on the left only.

Alert cyclists that you are passing.

Point out or announce road hazards.

Get completely off the road if you stop.

Signal your intentions (use hand or verbal signals.)

Appendix B:

Sources of Information

Bicycle Touring

League of American Wheelmen
Suite 209
6707 Whitestone Road
Baltimore, MD 21207
301-944-3399

Southern Bicycle League
Freewheelin'
P.O. Box 29474
Atlanta, GA 30359

Georgia Tourist Information

Atlanta Convention & Visitor Bureau
233 Peachtree Street, N.E.
Suite 200
Atlanta, GA 30043

Chickamauga National Military Park
P.O. Box 2128
Fort Oglethorpe, GA 30742

Cyclorama
Grant Park
Georgia and Cherokee Aves., S.E.
Atlanta, GA 30315
404-624-1071

Georgia Dept. of Industry and Trade
P.O. Box 1776
Atlanta, GA 30301

Georgia Dept. of Natural Resources
Parks, Recreation, and Historic Sites Division
Floyd Tower East, Suite 1352
205 Butler Street, S.E.
Atlanta, GA 30334
404-656-4DNR

Georgia Dept of Transportation
Steven L. Yost
2 Capitol Sq., Rm. 345
Atlanta, GA 30334
404-656-5351

Georgia State Capitol
Capitol Hill
Washington Street
Atlanta, GA 30334
404-656-2844

Kennesaw Mountain National Battlefield Park
Old Highway 41 and Stilesboro Road
Marietta, GA 30061
404-427-4686

Stone Mountain State Park
Highway 78
Stone Mountain, GA 30086
404-469-9831

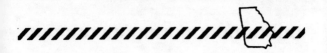

Chambers of Commerce Located Along the Route

Atlanta Chamber of Commerce
1300 North Omni International
P.O. Box 1740
Atlanta, GA 30303

Burke County Chamber of Commerce
c/o Lakeview Inn, Hwy 25 S
Waynesboro, GA 30830

Calhoun - Gordon County Chamber of
    Commerce
102 Court St.
Calhoun, GA 30701

Cartersville - Bartow County Chamber of
    Commerce
3 Dixie Ave.
P.O. Box 307
Cartersville, GA 30120

Covington - Newton County Chamber of
    Commerce
1121 Floyd St.
P.O. Box 168
Covington, GA 30209

Dalton - Whitfield County Chamber of
    Commerce
524 Holiday Dr.
P.O. Box 99
Dalton, GA 30720

//////////////////////////////.

Eatonton - Putnam County Chamber of
    Commerce
105 Sumter St.
P.O. Box 656
Eatonton, GA 31024

Greater Fort Oglethorpe Area Chamber of
    Commerce
P.O. Box 2263
Fort Oglethorpe, GA 30742

Louisville - Jefferson County Chamber of
    Commerce
P.O. Box 24
Louisville, GA 30434

Madison - Morgan County Chamber of
    Commerce
120 Main St.
P.O. Box 826
Madison, GA 30650

Marietta - Cobb County Chamber of
    Commerce
240 Interstate North Parkway
Marietta, GA 30065-2429

Milledgeville - Baldwin County Chamber of
    Commerce
130 Jefferson St.
P.O. Box 751
Milledgeville, GA 31061

Millen - Jenkins County Chamber of
    Commerce
200 Southside Cotton Ave.
Millen, GA 30442

Ringgold - Catoosa County Chamber of
 Commerce
303 Nashville St.
P.O. Box 52
Ringgold, GA 30736

Sandersville - Washington County Chamber
 of Commerce
P.O. Box 582
Sandersville, GA 31082

Savannah Area Chamber of Commerce
301 W. Broad St.
Savannah, GA 31499

Screven County - Sylvania Chamber of
 Commerce
101 S. Main Street
Sylvania, GA 30467

Statesboro - Bulloch County Chamber of
 Commerce
323 S. Main St.
Statesboro, GA 30458

Walton County - Monroe Chamber of
 Commerce
323 W. Spring St.
P.O. Box 89
Monroe, GA 30655

Sue and William Bailey are native Georgians who live in North Georgia with their daughters Ellaine and Kathryn.

William Bailey is principal of Rabun Gap Community School and for the past ten years has been an adjunct professor at DeKalb Community College. He has taught high school and served as an assistant principal in the Fulton County School System and was an assistant professor of geography at Eastern Kentucky University. He holds bachelor's and master's degrees in geography from the University of Georgia. After serving in the U.S. Army in Viet Nam, he returned to graduate school and earned a Ph.D. degree in geography at the University of Tennessee.

Sue Bailey teaches music at the Rabun Gap Nacoochee School. She holds a B.F.A. degree in music performance from the University of Georgia where she also attended graduate school, studying music history. She has taught private piano for twenty years.

High school sweethearts, the Baileys were married in 1966. The family enjoys touring the United States by bicycle and automobile, and camping along the way.